JO DIXEY

STITCH
PEOPLE

JO DIXEY

STITCH PEOPLE

A 20-project guide to modern embroidery techniques

SEARCH PRESS

This edition published in Great Britain in 2017 by
Search Press Ltd
Wellwood
North Farm Road
Tunbridge Wells
Kent TN2 3DR
www.searchpress.com

© Jo Dixey and David Bateman Ltd 2017

All rights reserved. No part of this publication may be reproduced, stored in a retrieval system, or transmitted in any form or by any means, electronic, mechanical, photocopying, recording, or otherwise, without the prior written permission of the copyright holder.

ISBN: 978-1-78221-562-2

The Publishers and author can accept no responsibility for any consequences arising from the information, advice or instructions given in this publication.

Readers are permitted to reproduce any of the items in this book for their personal use, or for the purpose of selling for charity, free of charge and without the prior permission of the Publishers. Any use of the items for commercial purposes is not permitted without the prior permission of the Publishers.

Suppliers
If you have any difficulty in obtaining any of the materials and equipment mentioned in this book, then please visit the Search Press website for details of suppliers.
www.searchpress.com

This book was conceived, designed and produced by
David Bateman Ltd, 30 Tarndale Grove, Albany, Auckand, New Zealand
www.batemanpublishing.co.nz

Printed in China through Colorcraft Ltd, Hong Kong

CONTENTS

Foreword	7
Introduction	8
Equipment	10

PROJECTS

BEGINNER

'Hands Off' scarf — *fusible web appliqué, couched edge*	14
'Cartwheel and Splits' skirt — *back stitch on ready-made skirt*	18
'Waiting for Life to Happen' t-shirt — *fusible web appliqué, buttonhole stitch edge on a ready-made t-shirt*	22
'Family Love' child's dress — *simple dress making, chain stitch*	26
Shopping bag — *bag construction, stitched appliqué, back stitch*	32
'Wireless' needle case — *working with layers of fabric, running stitch and back stitch*	36
'Street Style' drawstring bag — *bag construction, back stitch*	40

INTERMEDIATE

'A Moment of Calm' cushion — *back stitch, running stitch, quilting, cushion construction*	46
Birthday cards — *split stitch, simple lettering*	52
'Cell Phone Blues' picture — *split stitch*	58

'Windows to the Soul' stitched mini panel — simple
long and short, no shading　　　　　　　　　　　　　　　　62

'Moving but Still' metal thread picture — couching
with metal thread　　　　　　　　　　　　　　　　　　　68

Seeding face picture — transferring a design using
tissue paper, seeding stitch　　　　　　　　　　　　　　　72

'Watch your Back' jacket — chain stitch, fusible web appliqué,
buttonhole stitch on ready-made jacket　　　　　　　　　　76

ADVANCED

'Shades of Green' book cover — construction of
a book cover, stem stitch, long and short stitch　　　　　　80

'Talk Talk Talk' phone case — satin stitch,
long and short stitch, simple construction　　　　　　　　　86

'Ouch' pin cushion — 2 colour long and short stitch,
couched lettering.　　　　　　　　　　　　　　　　　　　90

'Bus Queue' stitch sampler — surface stitch sampler　　　96

ADVANCED +

'Man in the Moon' brooch — Or Nue couching　　　　　104

'Stoney Faced' long and short picture — shaded long
and short stitch　　　　　　　　　　　　　　　　　　　110

Stitch gallery　　　　　　　　　　　　　　　　　　　116

FOREWORD

Embroidery is a permanent way to sketch out a design. Perceptions often put hand-stitching in the shadows, and it is thought of as an activity from 'days gone by'. Thanks to artists like Jo Dixey, who has formed a reputation as an avant-garde textile artist with her appliqué wall hangings, embroidery has become an artistic expression of ideas.

Rather than getting overly concerned with details of specific techniques, Jo encourages stitchers to find their own style by introducing them to her own unique, expressionistic, cartoon-like statements which resonate accents of graffiti artist Banksy and the humourous works of Eddie Harding.

Hopefully in this, Jo's first book, you will feel encouraged to pick up a needle and thread and make a statement of your own.

Brandon Mably, Studio Manager, Kaffe Fassett Studios

INTRODUCTION

Welcome to the fantastic world of embroidery. Whatever the reason you picked up this book, you are about to start on a journey that will help you tap into your creative side and enable you to create one-off pieces of art, embellish items of clothing and make beautiful gifts for your friends.

I started on this path at the age of eight. My mother and grandmothers were all involved in some way with fabric and thread, so my childhood was full of inspiration and I had access to endless materials to play with. This love of stitch progressed from my main leisure activity to my job, when I left school in 1991 and went to the Royal School of Needlework to train as an embroiderer.

Over the years since, I have witnessed the enjoyment others have found from learning to stitch. I have taught embroidery workshops for more than twenty years and the number of beginners seems to grow all the time.

This book is designed for those new to embroidery as well as those with some knowledge of hand stitching. The projects will introduce you to the main embroidery stitches and then expand your knowledge and give you confidence to use those stitches on your own creative pathways. The projects range from small embroidered cards to more complex pictures to hang on your wall. I hope there is something for everyone.

I am sure you have guessed by just flicking through these pages that I love people. I love the shapes of eyes, ears and feet. I am fascinated by how people interact with each other and how technology is changing that interaction. I often sketch people, or bits of people, and my embroidery always seems to be based on the human body.

Whatever subjects you love to work with, I hope you have as much fun with embroidery as I do. I just can't imagine a house without a needle and a pile of thread to hand.

Jo Dixey

EQUIPMENT

Hoops

Embroidery hoops are designed to hold your fabric taut while you embroider. This helps prevent wrinkles from forming around the stitched areas, as the stitches will be tighter than the fabric.

It is best to buy a hoop with a groove in the head of the screw, as this means you can tighten the screw with a screwdriver to hold it firm. And always use a hoop that is large enough to contain your complete design as this means you will avoid crushing your embroidery between the two circles of the hoop.

To put your fabric in the hoop you need to separate the two parts, placing the solid ring on the table. Place your fabric over this ring and push the upper ring, the one with the screw, on top. You will need to loosen the screw slightly so it will fit.

Then work your way around the hoop, pulling the fabric tight as you go. Tighten the screw on your hoop to hold the fabric in place – it should feel like a drum.

Threads

There are lots of different threads and they all give a slightly different look or feel to your embroidery. For this book, I have used commonly available threads: stranded cotton, No. 8 perle cotton and machine sewing thread.

Stranded cotton is a great thread because it can be used as a single strand for fine work or as multiple strands for thicker work. It is easy to obtain, low cost and comes in a great range of colours. I just love stranded cotton!

Perle cotton comes in different sizes; No. 8 is in the middle of the range and the most commonly used. It is a twisted thread with a lovely shine, and is good for embroidery as it can really give your stitches a lift.

Machine sewing thread is fine and strong, and so perfect for sewing your projects together.

Needles

There are a variety of needles for different types of embroidery. All the projects in this book use needles that have a point (counted thread embroidery uses blunt needles). Buy the best quality needles you can, as you will never be happy stitching with cheap needles.

Needles are designed to make a hole in the fabric large enough for the thread to go through easily. Therefore, they come in different sizes and with different shaped eyes for different thicknesses of thread. The easy guide is that your thread should pull smoothly through the eye of the needle, this means it's the correct size. For example, one strand of stranded cotton will fit in a size 10 embroidery needle (also known as a crewel needle).

For this book I have only used embroidery needles. These have a long oval eye so there is plenty of space for the thread to go through. They come in a large range of sizes also, which accommodate the different threads I have used.

Scissors

Sharp scissors are very important when you are stitching, and having scissors that are sharp all the way to the point is essential. I only use three types of scissors: large fabric scissors, small embroidery scissors for threads and paper scissors. I never use my fabric scissors for anything else but fabric – this keeps them sharp. I have two pairs of embroidery scissors, one for thread and one for when I need to cut tiny pieces of fabric. When you have a family, I find it best to have one colour of scissors for your embroidery/sewing work that no one touches without asking, then general house scissors that are a different colour. This makes it easier for children to learn which scissors they can use and which they can't.

Fabric

For this book I have used patchwork cotton, linen, silk and calico.

I use calico to support the fabric when I am doing lots of embroidery. Calico almost always comes with a dressing in it to make it stiff for dressmakers. This will need to be washed out before you use it for embroidery. The best way to do this is with a hot wash through your washing machine, and then iron the calico when it is still a bit damp. All other fabrics are fine to use without washing.

When you are starting out on your embroidery journey, it is best to use smooth fabrics. Some types of silk and linen have lumps in them called slubs, these are hard to stitch over so are best avoided when you are learning. If you do fall in love with a textured fabric try to draw your design so the slubs are outside the stitching area.

Iron-on interfacing

Iron-on interfacing is used when you want your fabric to be stiffer, for example in the drawstring bag project in this book. Interfacing comes in different weights, but I mostly use a lightweight interfacing.

One side of the interfacing has a fine layer of fabric glue. The fabric is placed onto this side of the interfacing and ironed. This causes the glue to melt and the interfacing is fixed to the fabric. It is best to iron with the fabric side up so that the interfacing itself does not melt from the heat of the iron.

Iron-on fabric stabilizer

This is similar to interfacing but much softer. The purpose of this product is to stabilize the fabric without making the fabric stiff, making it great for clothing. It comes in black and white so choose the best one for your fabric colour. When you are stitching onto a lightweight fabric this product helps prevent wrinkles forming around your embroidery.

Fusible web

Fusible web is a very fine layer of fabric glue backed with paper. You use this for appliqué, when you want to attach one fabric to another. The mirror image of the shape is drawn onto the paper, this is then ironed onto the reverse side of the fabric. The design is cut out and the paper peeled off. The shape, fabric-side up, is then ironed onto the background fabric. If you are doing lots of different shapes you can put a sheet of baking paper between the fabric and the iron to prevent any loose bits of glue getting stuck to your iron.

PROJECTS

I love scarves, winter or summer. They add a bit of colour and fun to your outfit as well as keeping you warm. I came across this beautiful hand-woven, hand-dyed Indian fabric and just had to make something out of it for this book. I have chosen bright printed cotton for the hands to contrast with the uneven dye of the background fabric. You could use any fabric you love, or you could use a scarf you already have and jazz it up with some hand prints.

'HANDS OFF' SCARF

FINISHED SIZE
193 x 23cm (76 x 9in)

WHAT YOU NEED
Background fabric, 200cm x 55cm (79" x 21½in), the best fabric would be medium thickness

4 squares of fabric, 25cm (10in) square, the best fabric would be shirt weight fabric

4 squares of fusible web, 25cm (10in) square

Stranded cotton, the colour can either contrast or match your hand fabrics

Size 10 embroidery needle

Size 3 embroidery needle

Sewing machine

STITCHES USED
Couching

Backstitch or machine

TECHNIQUES
Appliqué using iron-on fusible web

INSTRUCTIONS

1. Cut your scarf fabric into 2 pieces 200cm (79in) long x approx. 27cm (10½in) wide.

2. Trace the hand print design on page 17 onto the paper side of the fusible web. You will need to trace as many hands as you want on your scarf. I have used four.

3. Iron each piece of fusible web onto the back of the fabric you are using for the hand prints [**A**].

A

> So many hands had been part of making this fabric, that it seems only right that I appliqué hand prints onto it. Appliqué is the technique of attaching a shape cut from one fabric to a background of another fabric. I have used fusible web to make the appliqué stronger for wearing and washing and edged the hand prints with a line of couching; this gives a nice solid line around the prints so they stand out well.

B

C

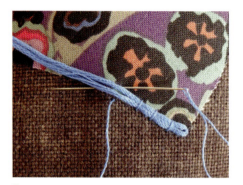

D

E

F

4. Cut out the hand shapes [**B**].

5. Peel the paper off and place the fabric hands onto one of your scarf lengths, fusible web-side down. I have put 3 hands at one end and 1 at the other.

6. When you are happy with the placement, iron in place [**C**].

7. Cut a length of stranded cotton 240cm (94½in) long. Fold in half.

8. Using a single thread of the same colour of stranded cotton and the size 10 needle, couch a line around the edge of each hand. The couching line will cover the edge of the fabric. To start, bring your needle up through the folded loop and do a stitch over the fold, then couch the 2 strands together. This makes the start of your couching neat [**D**].

9. When you have couched all around the hand shape, thread the 2 ends of the stranded cotton into the size 3 needle and pull them through to the back of the fabric. Cut these ends to about 3cm (1¼in) and stitch down to the back of the fabric.

10. When all the hands have been edged, pin the 2 pieces of scarf fabric right sides together and sew around 1cm (½in) from the edge leaving a 10cm (4in) gap in the centre of one narrow end. You can do this by hand using back stitch or by machine.

11. Trim a small triangle off each corner without cutting your stitches. This helps reduce the bulk of fabric in the corner [**E**].

12. Turn your scarf right-side out, carefully pushing out the corners and making sure the edges are flat. Pin the gap closed and press the whole scarf.

13. Top stitch close to the edge, either by machine or using a running stitch. This will hold the scarf flat when you wear it [**F**].

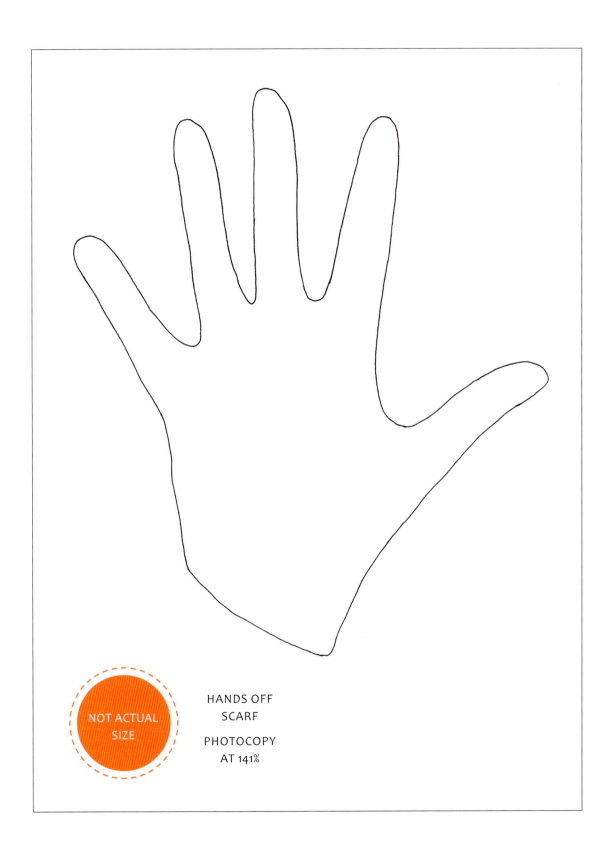

NOT ACTUAL SIZE

HANDS OFF SCARF

PHOTOCOPY AT 141%

When I talk to my daughter Morgan about my being nervous giving a talk or going to a meeting, she always tells me it will be alright if I enter the room doing a cartwheel that ends in the splits! This scenario is never likely to happen because my bottom has never been higher than my head, but I thought that I could embroider the action of a cartwheel to splits around a skirt, which might have the same confidence-boosting effect.

BEGINNER

'CARTWHEEL & SPLITS' SKIRT

STITCHED AREA
Will depend on the size of the skirt

WHAT YOU NEED
Skirt
No. 8 perle cotton thread
Size 5 embroidery needle
Iron-on fabric stabilizer
Transfer paper

STITCHES USED
Back stitch

TECHNIQUES
Transferring a design using transfer paper

INSTRUCTIONS

1. Measure the hem line of your skirt and divide this number in half. Enlarge the design on page 21 to match this measurement. The design printed in the book is half your total design, so you will trace the design twice onto the skirt.

2. Trace the enlarged design onto tracing paper.

3. Iron a 25cm (10in) wide strip of fabric stabilizer onto the wrong side along the bottom edge of your skirt. This will support the fabric and help reduce any wrinkles when you stitch.

4. Mark the centre front of your skirt with a pin.

5. Transfer the design onto your skirt using transfer paper, matching the edge of the design with the centre of the skirt. Flip the design over and transfer the design to the other side, matching the two halves of the centre figure [A].

A

> You could use this design to decorate a skirt you make yourself, one you buy second hand or to make a new skirt look different.
>
> You will use back stitch for this project. This is a very simple stitch suitable for clothing as it is flat, so there are no loose threads to get caught.

PROJECT | SKIRT 19

B

C

D

E

6. The markings made with transfer paper are quite soft. You will be handling the fabric a lot while you are stitching the figures, so if you see the design lines fading use a coloured pencil to re-draw them in before they completely disappear. My skirt is a dark colour so I used a white coloured pencil.

7. Start your thread in the normal way with a knot and two tiny back stitches, the knot is then cut off [B]. The tiny stitches will be covered over with the main back stitch [C].

8. Work back stitch along all your design lines, completing each figure before you move onto the next [D].

9. To reduce the bulk of thread, when you come to the end of your thread or the end of a line, turn your work to the wrong side and finish your thread by threading it through the back of the stitches for about 3cm (1¼in). Cut the remainder of the thread [E].

If you start your thread with 2 tiny stitches and finish by threading through the back, the extra bulk on the back of the work will be in two different areas and keep the front flat and the back neat.

10. When you have completed all the figures, iron your skirt; you are then ready to go.

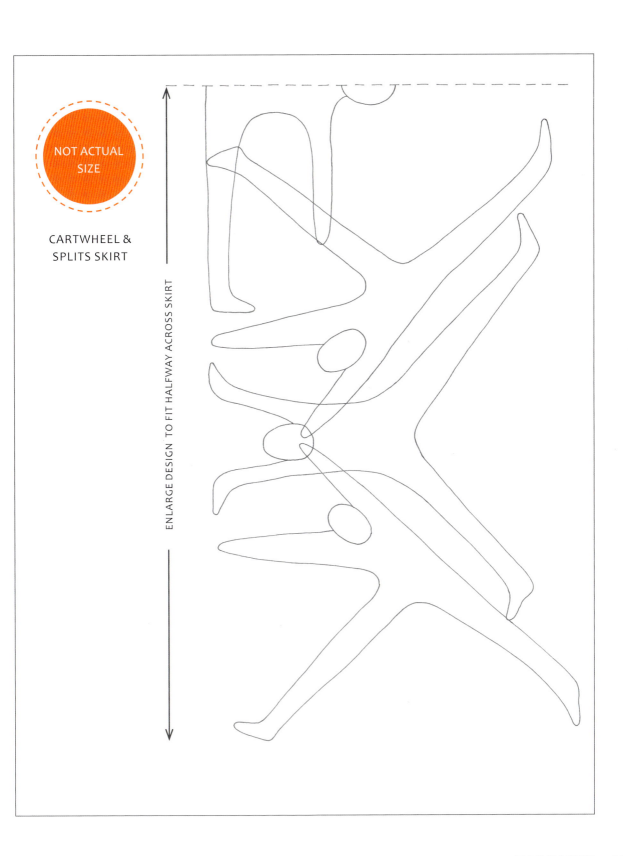

The design for this project came from a drawing I did of a teenager sitting at a skate park. I don't think I saw him skate at all that day, he looked like he was just waiting for something. Who knows what that something was? Maybe even he didn't know.

'WAITING FOR LIFE TO HAPPEN' T-SHIRT

STITCHED AREA
30 x 19cm (11¾ x 7½in)

WHAT YOU NEED
T-shirt

Small scraps of fabric, I used patchwork fabric

Fusible web

Size 10 embroidery needle

Stranded cotton to match T-shirt

Tracing paper

STITCHES USED
Buttonhole stitch

TECHNIQUES
Appliqué using iron-on fusible web

INSTRUCTIONS

1. Enlarge the design on page 25 and trace it onto a piece of tracing paper. You will need this tracing later to help with placing the fabric pieces. I have chosen to have just the one figure sitting at the bottom of my T-shirt, but you can change the size of the design and have two smaller figures if you wish.

2. Trace each section of the design onto the paper-side of your fusible web. Leave a gap between each one so you can cut them out easily.

3. Cut out each section of fusible web, leaving some space all around [**A**]. Iron these pieces to the reverse side of your fabric pieces. This ensures the fusible web goes right up to the edge of the cut-out fabric pieces and helps prevent the fabric from fraying [**B**].

A

B

> Appliqué is a great way to personalise a garment. In the 'Hands Off' scarf I used couching around the fabric. In this project I am using buttonhole stitch, a flat stitch which holds down the fabric well without creating texture.

BEGINNER

C

D

E

F

4. Cut each fabric piece out, on the pencil line of the fusible web [C].

5. Peel the paper off each section and place onto the T-shirt, using the design you traced onto tracing paper earlier to check the position of each piece [D]. The final design will be a mirror image of the original design, so you will need to turn over your tracing paper.

6. When you are happy with your placement, iron the pieces in place.

7. Using 1 strand of your stranded cotton, work a buttonhole stitch around each section [E]. This will prevent the fabric lifting up at the edges as you wear and wash the T-shirt. It also gives an almost stained glass window effect to the figure [F].

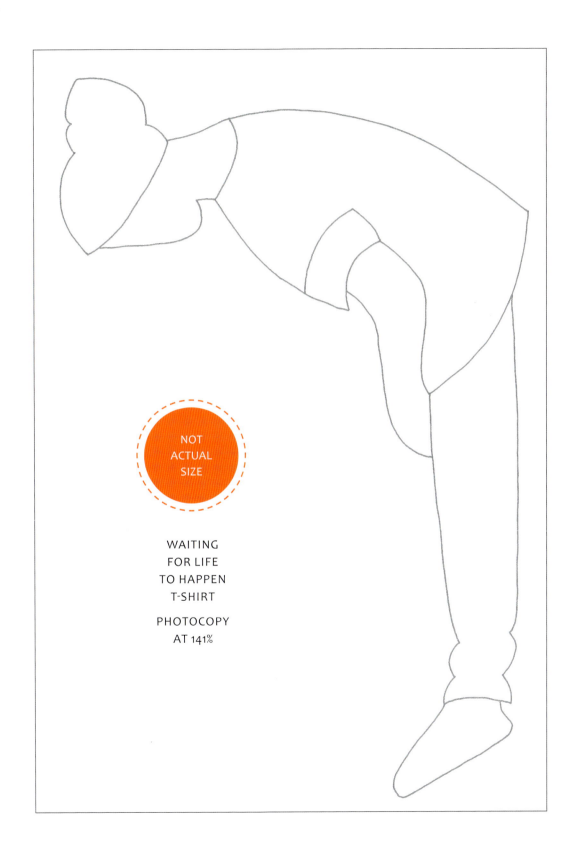

This project is a great introduction to chain stitch if you have not done it before, and also dressmaking if you want to give that a try. You could stitch this design onto a dress you purchased or were given to make it personal to you. Or you can have a go at some simple dressmaking: I have used a sewing machine, but it is possible to make this small dress by hand using small running stitch or back stitch for all the seams.

'FAMILY LOVE' CHILD'S DRESS

FINISHED SIZE

Dress fits 2–3 year old, stitched area 23cm x 9cm (9 x 3½in)

WHAT YOU NEED

Dress fabric, 50 x 112cm (19¾ x 44in), I have used linen but cotton would be fine too

Strip of coloured cotton fabric, 10cm x 114cm (4 x 44¾in)

2.5cm (1in) wide elastic, 34cm (13½in) in length

Sewing thread to match fabrics

No. 8 perle cotton thread

Size 5 embroidery needle

Sewing machine

STITCHES USED

Chain stitch

TECHNIQUES

Simple dressmaking

INSTRUCTIONS

1. Take your 50cm (19¾in) of fabric and sew into a tube, down the shorter side; your seam allowance is 1cm (½in), selvedges together. The selvedge is the firm edge of the fabric, and often has the information printed on it about the fabric. You can either leave the selvedges on or trim them off and neaten the cut edge with a zig-zag stitch.

2. Using the arm hole pattern piece on page 30, line up the straight edge of the pattern with the seam on one side and the fold on the other [A]. Cut out the arm holes [B].

A

B

C

D

E

F

3. Make a casing along the top edges, between the armholes, to hold the elastic. Fold down a 0.5cm (¼in) of fabric and press [C], then fold down 3cm (1¼in) and press. Sew this casing top and bottom — this stops the elastic twisting when the dress is washed [D].

4. Cut 2 pieces of elastic 17cm (6¾in) long and thread through the casing, front and back. To do this, pin a safety pin through one end of the elastic and use that to feed the elastic through the casing [E]. When the end of the elastic is about to disappear into the casing hold it in place with a pin.

5. Secure the elastic at either end with a few rows of stitching [F].

6. Cut 2 strips of the coloured cotton fabric 5 x 85cm (2 x 33½in). Fold one strip in half along its length and press. Open the strip out again and fold the 2 edges into the centre and press along its length [G].

7. Fold this strip in half and mark the centre of its length with a pin [H].

G

H

I

J

8. Match the centre point of the strip to the centre of the armhole and pin in place. Sandwich the dress in the middle of the strip, the cut edge of the dress should be pushed up to the centre fold of the strip [I].

9. Sew the strip, close to the open edges, from one end to the other [J]. This neatens the arm hole and creates straps at the same time. Repeat for the other armhole. Tie a knot in the fabric at the end of the straps to create a neat end.

10. Hem your dress. Fold and press 1cm (½in) all around the bottom edge. Then fold 1cm (½in) again to enclose the raw edge. Stitch in place [K].

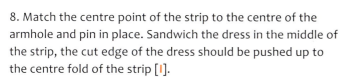

K

11. Trace the design on page 30 onto the bottom of the dress [L]. Use a light box or the window if you need to. If your fabric is thicker, you may need to use transfer paper.

12. Using two strands of No. 8 perle cotton, work chain stitch along all of your design lines [M]. You can't chain stitch around a sharp corner, so finish one line of chain stitch at the corner [N] and then start a new line, slightly crossing over the end of the first line. Do not worry too much about the back of your work, but try to keep it neat.

L

M

N

PROJECT | CHILD'S DRESS

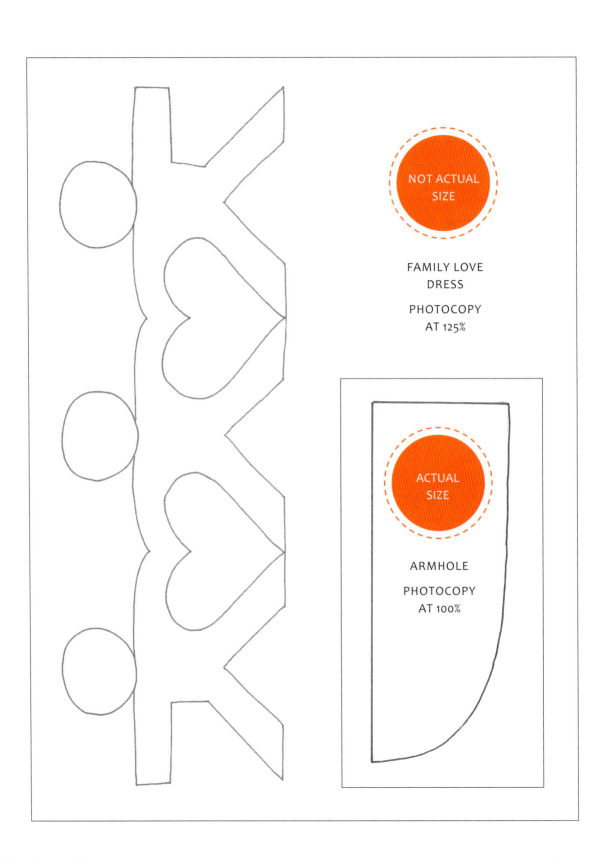

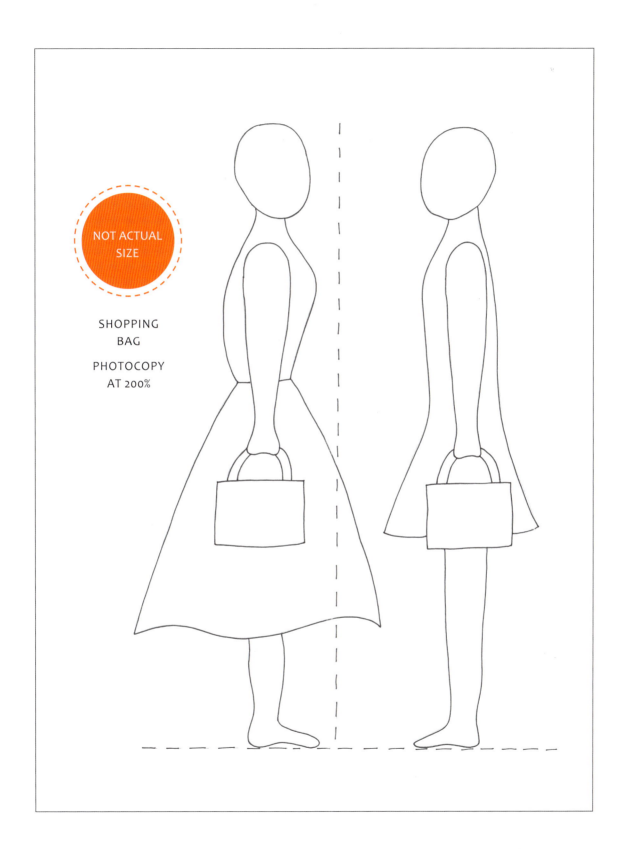

The world would be a better place if we all used less plastic bags. The easy answer is to make a cool shopping bag to carry with you when you go out. Make the lining as wild as you like, just to make you smile when you are unloading the purchases at home. This project repeats the back stitch you have already used on the 'Cartwheel and Splits' skirt and introduces another form of appliqué, where the edge of the fabric is folded under and then stitched down so the stitches do not show.

SHOPPING BAG

BEGINNER

FINISHED SIZE

39 x 33cm (15¼ x 13in), stitched area 33 x 21cm (13 x 8¼in)

WHAT YOU NEED

Natural-coloured linen fabric, 50 x 112cm (19¾ x 44in)

Cotton fabric for lining, 50 x 112cm (19¾ x 44in)

No. 8 perle cotton thread, black and colours to match your fabric scraps.

Purchased leather handbag handles — I use clip on ones

Cream sewing thread to match linen fabric

Size 5 embroidery needle

Size 10 embroidery needle

Sewing machine

STITCHES USED

Back stitch

Chain stitch

Slip stitch

TECHNIQUES

Appliqué

Simple bag construction

INSTRUCTIONS

1. Cut 2 pieces out of the linen 40 x 45cm (15¾ x 17¾in).

2. Take one piece and tack a line across the bottom (the narrower edge) 5cm (2in) from the edge, and then a second line up the centre of the fabric.

3. Enlarge the design on page 31 so the figures are 33cm (13in) high.

4. Transfer the design onto your linen so the figures are standing on the bottom tack line [**A**]. The best way to do this would be to use a light box or the window. Match the centre line marked on the design and your centre tack line to make sure your design is straight.

A

B

C

D

5. Iron interfacing onto the reverse side of the piece of linen with the design on it.

6. Using the size 5 embroidery needle, stitch the outlines of both figures with back stitch using black no. 8 perle cotton thread [**B**].

7. Stitch the handles of the handbags in your design using rows of chain stitch until the handle design is full, approximately 4 to 5 rows. Use a no. 8 perle cotton thread that matches your handbag fabric choice [**C, D**].

ADDING THE FABRIC FOR THE 'HANDBAGS'

1. Cut 2 pieces of fabric from your scraps measuring 7 x 5.5cm (2¾ x 2¼in).

2. Fold 1cm (½in) of fabric to the wrong side all around the piece and press with an iron [**E**].

3. Pin the fabric to the linen matching the folded edge to the design line you have drawn on [**F**].

4. Slip stitch the fabric in place using sewing thread to match the fabric and a size 10 embroidery needle [**G**].

E

F

G

34   STITCH PEOPLE

H

I

TO MAKE UP YOUR BAG

1. Pin the 2 pieces of linen, right sides together, and sew around 3 sides, leaving the top open. Leave a 1cm (½in) seam allowance. This can be done on a sewing machine if you have one or by hand using a small back stitch [H].

2. Cut 2 pieces of cotton lining fabric 40 x 45cm (15¾ x 17¾in).

3. Repeat step 1 with your lining fabric.

TO CREATE THE BASE OF THE BAG

1. Hold one bottom corner of your bag, right sides together. Separate the front and back of the bag. Pull apart to form a triangle, matching the bottom and side seams.

2. Mark a point 4cm (1½in) down from the top of the triangle. Draw a straight pencil line across the base of the triangle, through the point you have just marked [I]. Stitch on this pencil line [J].

Repeat this for the other corner of the bag and the two bottom corners of the lining [K].

J

TO FINISH THE BAG

1. Turn and press a 1cm (½in) seam allowance to the inside around the top of your bag and lining.

2. Turn your bag right side out and place your lining inside. Matching folded top edge and side seams.

3. Pin and then sew around the top edges of your bag to hold the bag and lining together, either by hand using slip stitch or using a straight machine stitch [L].

4. Attach your purchased handles.

K

L

Having a small case to hold a growing collection of needles is always useful and is a great project with which to start your embroidery journey. The sight of people looking at their smart phones is everywhere, and I love the idea of a design inspired by technology being used for hand craft.

'WIRELESS' NEEDLE CASE

FINISHED SIZE

11.5 x 10.5cm (4½ x 4¼in) (folded)

WHAT YOU NEED

Fine cream cotton fabric, voile or lawn, 30 x 60cm (11¾ x 23¾in)

White cotton flannel, 20 x 30cm (8 x 11¾in)

Black stranded cotton

Cream stranded cotton

White sewing thread for tacking

Size 10 embroidery needle

Small press stud

20cm (8in) embroidery hoop (optional)

STITCHES USED

Running stitch
Back stitch
Slip stitch

> This project introduces you to working with more than one layer of fabric. You will use a large running stitch (known as tacking/basting) to hold the layers together while you stitch. It is the layers of fabric that give the background of this project its texture.

INSTRUCTIONS

1. Cut 3 pieces of fine cream fabric, each 20 x 30cm (8 x 11¾in).

2. Trace the design on page 39 onto one piece of fabric, including the outside rectangle [A].

3. Pin the 3 layers of fabric together, with the design on the top. Work lines of large running stitch (also known as tacking) in a grid to hold the layers of fabric together. The rows of running stitch should be about 4cm (1½in) apart.

4. Using 1 strand of black stranded cotton, back stitch all the outlines of the figures [B]. Be careful not to pull your stitches too tight. You can put the fabric into a hoop to do this part if you wish to. (If you used a hoop for the back stitch, remove your fabric when you have finished as the next step is worked without a hoop so the fabric ripples slightly.)

A

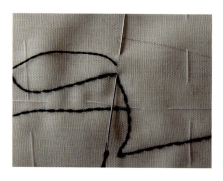

B

STITCH PEOPLE

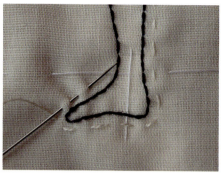

C

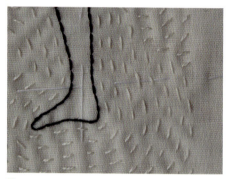

D

5. Using 1 strand of cream stranded cotton, stitch rows of small running stitch around your figures. Begin your rows about 0.3cm (⅛in) away from your black lines [C].

6. Work 2 rows around each figure first, then, keeping the rows evenly spaced, fill the whole area with rows of running stitch. Stop your running stitch each time you come to the outside rectangle that you traced on in step 2 [D].

7. Remove your tacking threads. These may have got caught up with your running stitch, if so, just snip the tacking thread close to where it is caught and give it a little pull to free it.

8. Take your piece of white cotton flannel and with right sides together pin the stitched piece to the flannel piece.

9. Sew around the line of the rectangle, using the edge of your running stitched area as a guide. Leave a gap where it is marked on the design. You can either hand sew using a small running stitch or use a sewing machine. Trim the excess fabric to about 1cm (½in) all around and trim the corners off, but not too close to your stitching.

10. Turn your needle case right side out. Carefully poke out corners and the side seams. Press.

11. Use slip stitch to close the gap you left for turning [E].

12. Work a small running stitch around the outside edge of your needle case [F]. This will hold all the layers together and help your case keep its shape.

13. Fold the needle case in half, so you have 3 figures on the front and one on the back. Stitch a line of cream running stitch along this fold line, working through all the layers. This will stop your outside and lining separating when you use your needle case.

14. Sew on a press stud to keep your needle case closed.

E

F

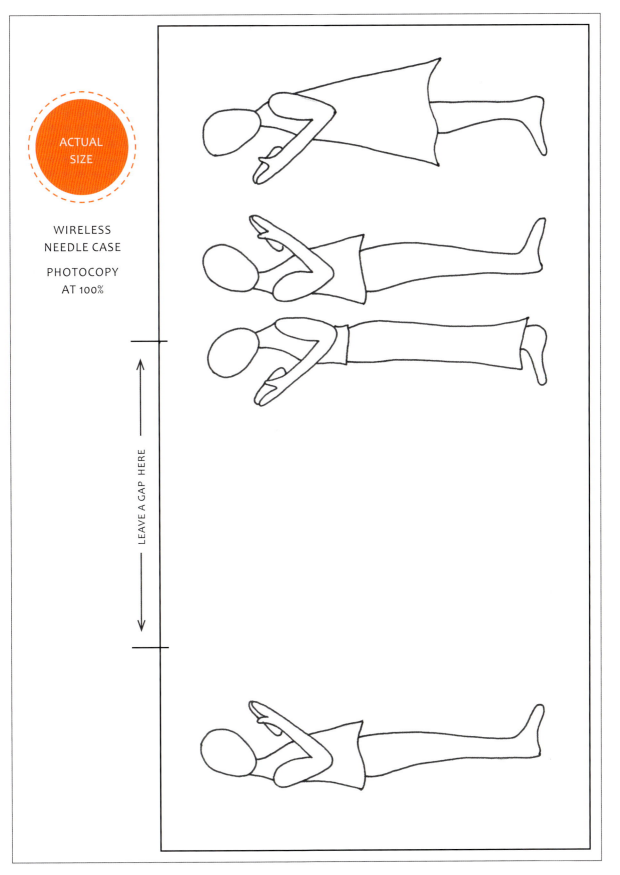

ACTUAL SIZE

WIRELESS NEEDLE CASE

PHOTOCOPY AT 100%

LEAVE A GAP HERE

PROJECT | NEEDLE CASE

I love sitting in public places and watching people; the different clothes, hair and how people interact is fascinating. There are a number of books and blogs dedicated to 'street style' now, so we can people-watch from the comfort of our own homes.

'STREET STYLE' DRAWSTRING BAG

BEGINNER

BAG SIZE

26 x 22cm (10¼ x 8¾in)

WHAT YOU NEED

Bag fabric, 40 x 90cm (15¾ x 35½in), I have used patchwork cotton

Lining fabric, 40 x 90cm (15¾ x 35½in), I have used patchwork cotton

Iron-on interfacing, 40 x 90cm (15¾ x 35½in)

No. 8 perle cotton thread

Size 5 embroidery needle

Transfer paper

Embroidery hoop, 20cm (8in)

STITCH USED

Back stitch

TECHNIQUES

Bag construction

Transferring design using transfer paper or a light box

The embroidery on this drawstring bag shows you that a stitch that is normally only used as an outline can also be very effective as a filling stitch. I have used back stitch which, when used as a filling stitch, gives beautiful detail to the solid areas.

INSTRUCTIONS

1. Iron the interfacing to the back of your bag fabric. Work a row of running stitch around the outside edge to prevent the 2 layers separating while you stitch.

2. Draw a rectangle 56.5 x 30cm (22¼ x 11¾in) onto this piece of fabric, drawing the top of the rectangle at the top of the fabric so you have extra material to fit in your hoop.

The design on this bag is near the bottom so you need the extra material to allow you to centre the design in the hoop. This fabric is later cut off.

3. Tack a line 2cm (¾in) up from the bottom line of the rectangle. This is to help keep your people in a straight line [A].

4. Transfer the designs on page 45 onto the fabric using a light box or transfer paper. The people can be placed wherever you like along the tack line.

5. Place the fabric into your hoop, with one figure in the centre. Work your way around the hoop, pulling the fabric tight. Now tighten the screw on your hoop to hold the fabric in place. Your fabric should feel like a drum.

A

B

C

D

E

F

6. Work back stitch along all your design lines, starting and finishing your thread with 2 tiny back stitches [**B, C**].

7. Use the diagram and finished image to help work rows of back stitch to fill in the solid areas, working from the outside of the area inwards [**D, E**].

8. When you have completed each figure move the hoop and place a new figure in the centre. When all the figures have been stitched you are ready to make the bag.

MAKING THE BAG

1. Using the pattern template on page 44, cut a base from the bag fabric with interfacing ironed on the back.

2. Fold this circle in half and place a pin at each end of the fold and then fold again, matching these pins and putting more pins at each end of the fold. You now have 4 quarters marked.

3. Cut out your bag, along the pencil lines you drew on earlier in step 2.

4. Fold this rectangle in half, right sides together, and sew along the short sides with a seam allowance of 0.5cm (¼in).

5. Keeping the right side to the inside, mark the 4 quarters of the base of this rectangle. One marker is the seam, fold the bag in half with the seam on one side and place a pin opposite the seam. Fold the bag in half again, lining up the pin and the seam and place 2 more pins at each fold.

6. With right sides together, pin the base to the bag, matching the quarter-markers first and then putting more pins in between [**F**].

7. Sew around the edges by hand or using a machine, allowing a 0.5cm (¼in) seam [**G**].

8. Cut a 56.5 x 30cm (22¼ x 11¾in) rectangle of lining fabric, and a base circle using the template on page 44.

G

H

9. Sew the lining together in the same way as you did the outside of the bag.

10. Turn the bag right side out and place the lining inside.

11. Turn a 1cm (½in) seam down around the top edge of the bag and the lining.

12. Pin the bag and lining together around this top edge and stitch as close as you can to the top [H].

13. Cut 2 strips of bag fabric, measuring 25 x 5cm (10 x 2in).

14. Along the 2 long sides, fold over 1cm (½in) of the fabric to the wrong side. Hem the 2 short ends by folding the edge in by 1cm (½in) and then folding again to conceal the raw edge [I]. Sew in place close to the open edge.

I

15. Measure 5cm (2in) down from the top of the bag and pin one of these strips in place, parallel with the top edge. Measure 5cm (2in) from one end of the strip and pin the next strip in place, also parallel with the top edge. These will hold the draw strings [J]. Machine or hand stitch these strips in place along the top and bottom edges.

16. Cut 2 strips 5 x 80cm (2 x 31½in) out of the lining fabric for the draw strings.

17. Fold in 1cm (½in) along each of the long edges and then fold the whole strip in half along its length. Stitch close to the open edge. Do the same with the second strip.

18. Pin a safety pin in the end of one strip and thread it around the bag, through the 2 channels created in step 15. Take the second strip, and starting at the opposite end of the first channel, thread around the bag. You will have 2 cut ends on each side of the bag [K].

19. Tie a knot in each end of the strips and then tie the two ends together.

J

K

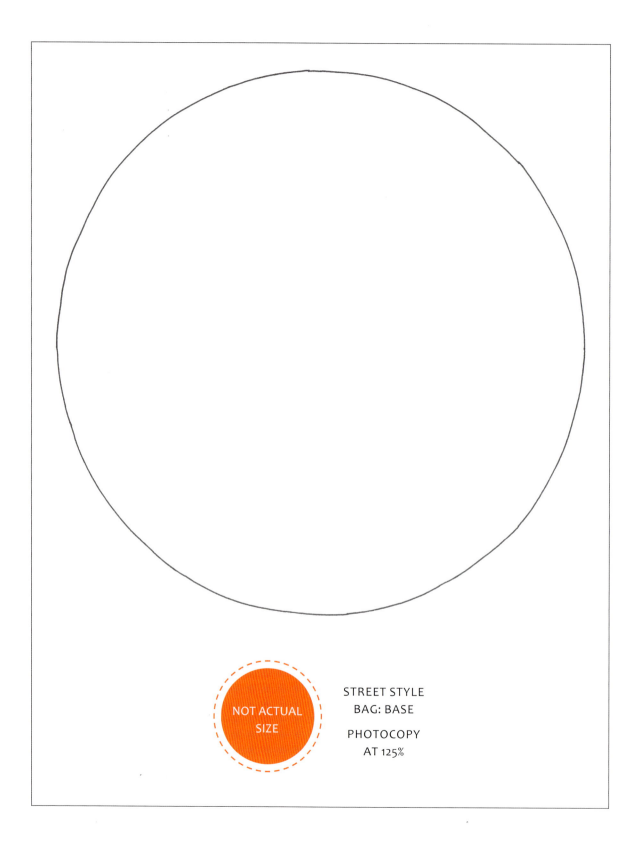

STREET STYLE BAG: BASE

PHOTOCOPY AT 125%

Although colour is fantastic, sometimes it's nice to do a piece that is a single shade just to give yourself a rest. This project introduces you to quilting, a technique of sandwiching layers of fabric and batting/wadding together, then stitching to create a soft, puffy surface. This cushion is cream on cream, which allows the slightly quilted texture to show.

'A MOMENT OF CALM' CUSHION

INTERMEDIATE

CUSHION SIZE
40 x 40cm (15¾ x 15¾in)

WHAT YOU NEED
Cream patchwork cotton fabric, 100 x 112cm (39¼ x 44in)

Cotton batting, 50 x 50cm (19¾ x 19¾in)

Cream quilting thread

Size 10 embroidery needle

Cream sewing thread

White zip, 30cm (11¾in)

Cushion inner, 40 x 40cm (15¾ x 15¾in)

Sewing machine

STITCHES USED
Tacking

Back stitch

Running stitch

TECHNIQUES
Inserting a zip

Transferring the design by tracing through the fabric

INSTRUCTIONS

1. Copy and enlarge the design on page 51 so it measures 25cm (10in) across. (NB: the design is not square).

2. Cut 2 pieces of cotton fabric 50 x 50cm (19¾ x 19¾in).

On the right side of your fabric trace the design onto the centre of one piece of your fabric using a 2H pencil [**A**]. This ensures you will not have too dark a pencil line to cover. If your fabric is too thick, use a light box or the window.

A

This project would be ideal for a bed cushion where it wouldn't get much wear. The repeating design gives you the opportunity to practice quilting on one project. By the time you have stitched all the figures you will be on your way to being a confident quilter.

B

3. Sandwich the piece of batting between the 2 squares of cotton (the square with the design on face up). Work lines of tacking (large running stitch) in a grid to hold the layers of fabric together. The rows of tacking should be about 4cm (1½in) apart. This will stop the layers moving while you quilt [B].

4. Using your cream quilting thread, work a back stitch along all the design lines [C]. Because you have a layer of batting between your 2 layers of cotton you can hide a knot in this inner layer to start your thread.

To do this, tie a small knot in the end of your thread, slide your needle through the top layer of cotton fabric and into the batting, coming up at the point you wish to start stitching. Give your thread a firm tug, and the knot will pull through the cotton fabric and get caught in the batting.

C

5. To finish your thread, you can do a small stitch on top of your last back stitch and then slide the needle and thread through the batting and top layer of cotton about 5cm (2in) from your end point, then cut your thread. This length of thread is then held in place by the rows of running or back stitches [D].

6. Using cream quilting thread, stitch rows of small running stitch around your figures [E]. Begin your rows about 0.3cm (⅛in) away from your back stitch lines. Work 1 row around each figure first, then, keeping the rows evenly spaced, fill the whole area with rows of running stitch. I finished my stitching with 3 rows around the outside edge of the figures, and then filled the spaces between the figures [F].

D

E

F

7. Due to the shape of the figures, there are indents in the outside edge of the design. I have worked 'V' shapes of running stitch in these spaces to make it look like the running stitch continues to flow beyond the design's edge [G].

8. Remove your tacking threads. These may have got caught up with your running stitch; if so, just snip the tacking thread close to where it is caught and give it a little pull to free it.

Now you are ready to make your quilted panel into a cushion.

G

PROJECT | CUSHION

H

I

J

HOW TO MAKE YOUR CUSHION

1. First make the back of your cushion by cutting two pieces of cotton fabric 42 x 30cm (16½ x 11¾in). A zip will be inserted between these 2 pieces (i.e. centred across the back of the cushion) so the cushion cover can be removed for washing.

2. Pin these pieces right sides together and sew a 6cm (2¼in) long seam at each end of the longer side of the fabric. You can either use a sewing machine or back stitch by hand. Tack the remaining centre section of the seam [H]. Press the seam open.

3. On the back, pin your zip, right side down with the teeth centred over the tacked seam. Sew the zip in place as close to the teeth as you can, either by machine or using back stitch by hand. Turn to the right side and remove your tacking [I].

4. Trim your quilted panel so it measures 42 x 42cm (16½ x 16½in). Make sure your design is in the centre.

5. Pin your quilted panel (the cushion front) and the cushion back (with zip inserted) right sides together and sew all around the edge, either by machine or by hand using back stitch. Have the zip slightly open when you do this to make it easier to turn inside out at the end.

6. Trim the extra fabric from the cushion back.

7. Turn your cushion right side out and push out the corners.

8. Insert your cushion pad [J].

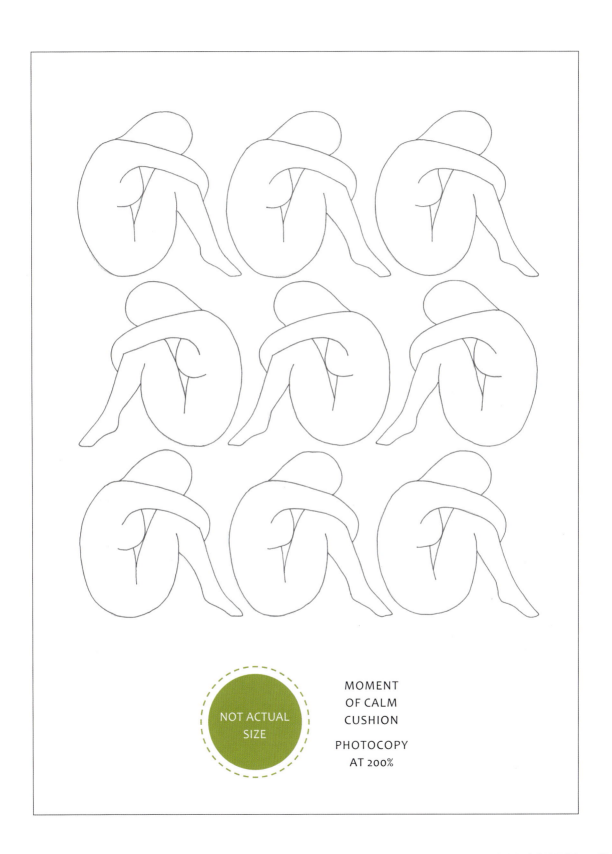

It's a great feeling to receive a greeting card that someone has made especially for you. I have designed these to be birthday cards, but you could change the words underneath or miss them out entirely. I have used just one stitch, split stitch, in this project which gives a lovely sense of movement when worked in rows very close together. The way the light falls on the stitching makes it look like you have used shaded thread.

BIRTHDAY CARDS

INTERMEDIATE

STITCHED AREA
10.5 x 6cm (4¼ x 2¼in)

WHAT YOU NEED
Background fabric, 15 x 10cm (6 x 4in); I have used silk but you can use cotton or anything you like the colour of, just be sure that it is not too thick

Washed calico, 25 x 25cm (10 x 10in)

Stranded cotton

Size 10 embroidery needle

Embroidery hoop, 20cm (8in)

Card, to mount the embroidered panels on

STITCHES USED
Split stitch

Back stitch

TECHNIQUES
Transferring design

Simple mounting

INSTRUCTIONS

1. Transfer one of the designs on pages 56–57 onto the centre of your background fabric, either by tracing it with a pencil through a light box or using transfer paper [A].

2. Using back stitch, either by hand or with a sewing machine, sew your background fabric onto the centre of your calico square. This double layer of fabric supports the stitching and saves you from wasting your fabric as it is the calico that goes into the hoop.

3. Place the calico in your hoop and work your way around, pulling the fabric tight. Now tighten the screw on your hoop to hold the fabric in place. Your fabric should feel like a drum.

A

> Split stitch is similar to back stitch with a bit of added texture. It is used again later in the book to support satin stitch and long and short.

B

NOTE: Each area of the figure – the legs, head, arms and clothing – is stitched separately, so it does not matter what order you stitch them in. The diagrams opposite show you the direction your rows need to go. Stitching the rows in this way helps to make the image look more realistic, e.g. the trousers look like they continue up under the jacket, the arm looks like it goes into the pocket.

4. Using a single strand of stranded cotton, begin with a row of split stitch along the outside edge of the area being worked (in [B] I have started with the leg).

Work rows of split stitch next to each other, working into the centre of the shape until the whole area is full. Then move onto the next area [C, D].

The laces of the boot are worked with long stitches over the top of the split stitch.

5. Using back stitch, stitch in the words following the pencil lines you have drawn on [E]. You can jump the thread across the back of the fabric from letter to letter. Be careful not to pull them too tight.

C

E

D

54   STITCH PEOPLE

F

6. Remove the fabric from the hoop. Tack a rectangle around the embroidery 10 x 6cm (4 x 2¼in) [F].

7. Trim the excess fabric away to leave at least 1cm (½in) all around the tacking line.

8. Fold the fabric on the tack line, pin and press.

9. With a single strand of stranded cotton in a contrast colour, work a running stitch all around the edge to hold the folded fabric in place. Remove the tacking thread [G].

10. Cut a piece of card measuring 15 x 21cm (6 x 8¼in). Fold in half to create a greeting card.

11. Place the embroidered piece in the centre of the card. Using a single thread, work a single stitch in each corner, knotting the two ends together on the inside of the card. Secure with a small piece of masking tape [H].

G

H

DIAGRAM SHOWING DIRECTION OF ROWS OF SPLIT STITCH.

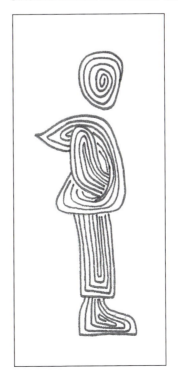
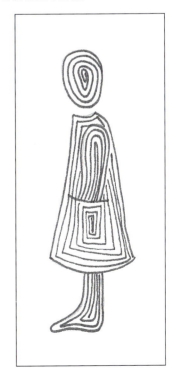

PROJECT | BIRTHDAY CARDS

BIRTHDAY BOOTS

PHOTOCOPY AT 100%

BIRTHDAY DRESS

PHOTOCOPY AT 100%

PROJECT | BIRTHDAY CARDS

It seems sometimes that everywhere you look people are glued to their phones, constantly connected to the world. Stranded cotton is shiny so when you change the direction of the stitching the light falls on it in a different way, creating movement on the flat surface of embroidery. In my mind this resembles the energy and information running around people's heads while they are on the phone.

'CELL PHONE BLUES' PICTURE

STITCHED AREA

10 x 7 cm (4 x 2¾in)

WHAT YOU NEED

Main fabric, 20 x 20cm (8 x 8in); I have used silk but any smooth fabric would be fine

Calico, 50 x 50cm (19¾ x 19¾in)

5 shades of blue stranded cotton

Size 10 embroidery needle

Embroidery hoop, 25cm (10in)

STITCHES USED

Split stitch

TECHNIQUES

Transferring design using transfer paper, or by tracing through the fabric with a light box

INSTRUCTIONS

1. Transfer the design on page 61 onto your background fabric. If you are using a pale fabric you can trace through or if your fabric is dark you can use transfer paper.

2. By hand or machine, sew your background fabric onto the centre of your calico square. You need a double layer of fabric to support the stitching and this also prevents your good fabric going into the hoop.

3. Place the calico in the hoop then work your way around, pulling the fabric tight. Now tighten the screw on the hoop to hold the fabric in place. Your fabric should feel like a drum.

4. Each area of this design is worked using rows of split stitch, working from the outside of each area into the centre. The diagram on page 62 gives you an idea of the direction of the rows.

5. Start the face by stitching the eyes, eye brows, lips and nostril. This ensures these are the correct shape and size, before you stitch in the rest of the face [A].

A

INTERMEDIATE

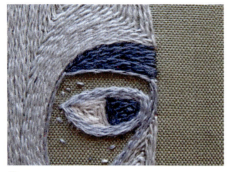

B

D

E

F

C

6. Start to fill the rest of the face. Work 3 rows of split stitch around the eyes and lips first [B]: This ensures there are smooth rows of stitching around these features of the face. Then work from the outside of the area towards the centre.

7. The rows of the phone are worked by interrupting the rows along the outline of the fingers [C]. By working in this way, it looks like the phone goes behind the hand [D].

8. When working the hand, start and end each row unevenly at the wrist end of the hand [E]. If you worked a straight line of stitches across the area it would look like the hand had been chopped off; having an uneven edge of stitches makes it look like the hand continues onto an arm that is not seen [F].

9. Use the photograph on page 60 to help you choose which shade of thread to use for different areas of the face. The darkest is for the phone, the next darkest for the lips, eye brows, underside of the nose and pupil of the eye. The next 3 shades are used on the face, with the lightest shade for the 'whites' of the eyes.

10. When you have finished your piece, you can take it to a framer to frame, or it could be made into a phone cover.

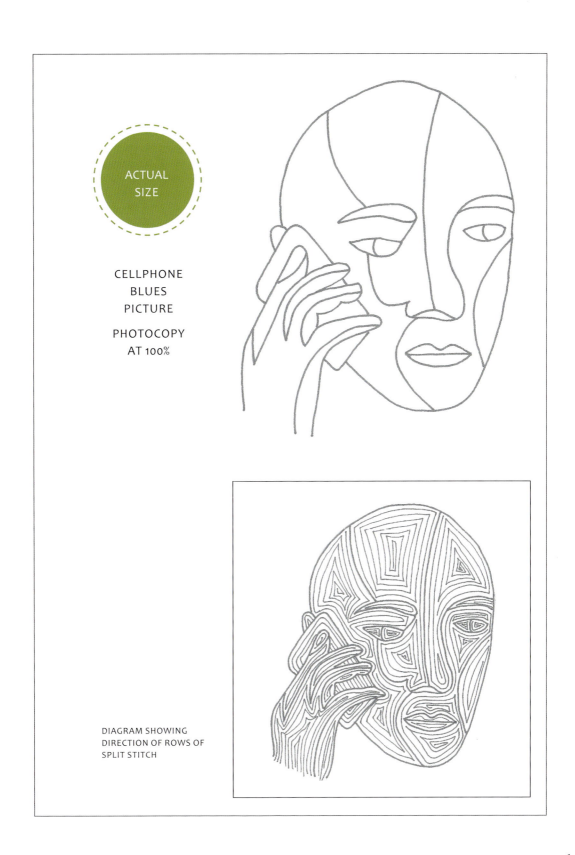

Eyes are often called the windows to the soul; you can often tell the true mood of someone by looking them in the eye. This panel could be used on a card or mounted in a frame. These small eyes are an introduction to long and short stitch. There is no change of colour within the areas of long and short so you can concentrate on the stitch, which is a great way to learn before you start to include shading.

INTERMEDIATE

'WINDOWS TO THE SOUL' STITCHED MINI PANEL

STITCHED AREA

5 x 3cm (2 x 1¼in)

WHAT YOU NEED

Calico, 35 x 35cm (13¾ x 13¾in)

Stranded cotton, 1 colour for the background and 3 shades for the eye

Size 10 embroidery needle

Small embroidery hoop, 20cm (8in)

STITCHES USED

Long and short stitch

Split stitch

Satin stitch

INSTRUCTIONS

1. Place the calico into your hoop and work your way around the hoop, pulling the fabric tight. Now tighten the screw on the hoop to hold the fabric in place. Your fabric should feel like a drum.

2. Trace the eye design on page 67 onto the calico [**A**]. You can do this by holding the design under the hoop, as you should be able to see through the calico.

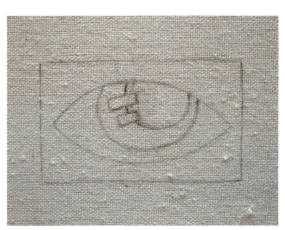

A

Long and short stitch is often called 'needle painting' because of its smooth surface and the stitch's ability to change colours making it similar to painting. The stitches are longer than those used with other embroidery so it takes a while to feel comfortable. Before you start this project, I recommend that you read through the long and short stitch instructions on page 126–127.

B

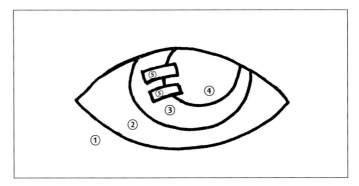

C

3. Start with the background colour. Using 1 strand of stranded cotton, work a split stitch around the outside edge of your rectangle [**B, C**].

4. The long and short stitches on this piece are worked from top to bottom, parallel with the short sides of the rectangle. Draw some pencil lines onto the calico to ensure your stitches stay straight [**D**].

5. Starting from the top centre the first few stitches are satin stitch (that is a single stitch from top to bottom) as the area is very narrow. The guide is, if an area is narrower than a short stitch of your long and short, i.e. about 1cm (½in), the area becomes satin stitch.

D

Long and short stitch is worked from the background to the foreground (or the part of the pattern most 'behind' to the most 'on top'). For this piece the order of work will be:

① background

② white of the eye

③ iris

④ pupil

⑤ highlight in the eye

(see diagram above).

Each area has a split stitch edge around it when the edge is 'on top'. This split stitch is covered up with long and short stitches. Almost all edges within a long and short design will have a split stitch, and it is just when they get to that split stitch that you see the secret to the success of the design. The edge gets its split stitch once the area behind that edge has been stitched; this keeps the edges crisp and the design accurate.

E

STITCH PEOPLE

F

G

As you work along this top edge, the area gets wider and you will need to start working shorter stitches which you shall mix in with longer ones. All your stitches will be slightly different lengths, the long stitches being about 1cm (½in) and the short ones being about 0.5cm (¼in). Your needle will come up through the fabric and down over the split stitch [E].

6. Once you have completed a full first row you can move on and work a second row [F], this time bringing your needle up through the stitch in the first row and down into the fabric. All your rows are now worked in the same way as a second row. The section in the bottom centre will be satin stitch as it becomes narrow [G]. Continue working rows until the background is full [H].

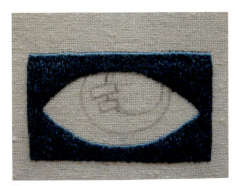

H

7. Change to the lightest of your eye colours and work a split stitch round the edge of the eye. Only split stitch where the white of the eye is on the top of the background [I].

8. Starting at the top, work long and short stitches to fill the white of the eye. Where the eye narrows at either end this will become satin stitch [J, K].

I

J

K

PROJECT | MINI-PANEL

L

M

N

9. When the white of the eye has been filled [L], change to the middle eye colour and work a split stitch around the eye's iris. There is a short piece at the top where the iris is on top of the background, and all round the edge where it is on top of the white of the eye.

10. Fill this area with long and short stitch, working from the top [M].

11. Change to the darkest eye colour for the pupil. Split stitch around the outside edge and fill with long and short [N].

12. The final areas to be filled are the highlights on the eye. Work these in the lightest eye colour. Split stitch around the outside edge and fill using satin stitch, then bring your needle up just outside the top split stitch edge and go down over the bottom split stitch edge.

13. Cut out your stitched rectangle, leaving 1cm (½in) of calico all around [O].

14. Fold the calico along the edge of the embroidery and hold in place using small stitches that just catch the calico and the thread on the back of the stitches [P].

15. You could mount your embroidered piece onto a card, stitch a brooch pin to the back and wear it, or put it in a frame.

O

P

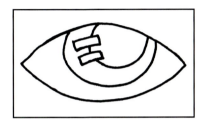

ACTUAL SIZE

WINDOWS
TO THE SOUL
STITCHED
MINI-PANEL

PHOTOCOPY
AT 100%

The light reflecting on metal thread changes as the direction of the thread changes; this creates an amazing sense of movement. The design of this calm, curled figure suggests stillness but the play of light on the thread gives the impression of movement. For this, the first metal thread project, I have used passing thread (made by a fine metal wire being wrapped around a cotton thread). This creates a firm thread that can be folded into any shape without showing its core. This is also the first project where rows of couching fill a space. When working couching in rows, always bring your needle up on the fabric side and then down next to the previous row — this pulls the rows closer together.

'MOVING BUT STILL' PICTURE

FINISHED FIGURE

6 x 6cm (2¼ x 2¼in)

WHAT YOU NEED

Calico, 35 x 35cm (14 x 14in)

Background fabric, 15 x 15cm (6 x 6in); I used a small scrap of green silk but any smooth fabric would work

No. 6 passing thread, 7m (23ft); I have used copper but it comes in different colours

Machine sewing thread to match the passing thread

Size 10 embroidery needle

Size 3 embroidery needle

Embroidery hoop, 20cm (8in)

STITCHES USED

Couching

INSTRUCTIONS

1. Trace the design from page 71 onto the background fabric either using a light box or window, or transfer paper if your fabric is dark or thick.

2. Sew your background fabric onto the centre of your calico square, by hand using back stitch or using a sewing machine. You need a double layer of fabric to support the stitching, and this also prevents your fabric going into the hoop [**A**].

3. Place the calico into your hoop, and working your way around, pull the fabric tight. Tighten the screw on the hoop to hold it in place. Your fabric should feel like a drum.

A

When you are couching in rows to fill an area, the thread stays attached to the reel until you have filled the area you are working on. Then the thread is cut. This ensures you do not waste any by over-estimating how much you need or, conversely, run out of thread and have to start a new thread halfway through an area.

INTERMEDIATE

B

C

D

4. You are now ready to start the couching. Use the sewing thread and the size 10 needle to couch over the passing thread to hold it in place [B]. Leaving a 4cm (1½in) length of passing hanging free, start stitching at the point where the head meets the arm. Work rows of couching side by side, working from the outside in. Turn your metal where the head joins the arm.

5. To turn the passing thread, you need to work a couching stitch at the end of the row, then bend the passing thread against this stitch and pinch [C]. You can use a pair of tweezers to do this.

6. When you have filled the head area, cut your passing thread, leaving 4cm (1½in) hanging free [D].

7. Next work the body, outside to inside as before. Start the couching at the point where the arm joins the leg, leaving a 4cm (1½in) length free.

The diagram opposite will help you with where the rows of couching will flow. The actual number of rows will differ for each person, as it depends on your stitch tension, but the lines on the diagram indicate the direction to lay the passing thread.

8. Due to the shape of the body design, you will have small areas that need to be filled in separately. Always remember to leave a 4cm (1½in) length of passing thread at the start and end of each area [E].

9. Once your whole figure has been completed, use a no. 3 needle to pull your start and finish ends through to the back of the fabric.

10. Couch these ends to the stitches on the reverse of the work [F].

E

F

70 STITCH PEOPLE

ACTUAL SIZE

MOVING
BUT STILL
PICTURE

PHOTOCOPY
AT 100%

DIAGRAM SHOWING DIRECTION OF ROWS OF COUCHING

This project introduces you to a new way of transferring a design onto fabric and a new stitch. The new method of transferring a design uses tacking through tissue paper and is used when you do not want a hard outline around the design. Because the design lines are tacked on, once the embroidery has been completed the tacking is removed and no-one would know it was ever there. I have used the same face design as the notebook cover to show how designs can look very different when worked in different techniques.

SEEDING FACE PICTURE

STITCHED AREA

19 x 13cm (7½ x 5in)

WHAT YOU NEED

Background fabric, 50 x 50cm (19¾ x 19¾in); I have used a plain patchwork weight cotton but a smooth silk work too

Calico, 50 x 50cm (19¾ x 19¾in)

Stranded cotton, dark colours work best

Sewing thread for tacking, any colour

Embroidery hoop, 25cm (10in)

Size 8 embroidery needle

White tissue paper

STITCHES USED

Tacking (large running stitch)

Running stitch

Seeding stitch

INSTRUCTIONS

1. Trace the design on page 85 on a piece of white tissue paper using a 2H pencil; this is a hard pencil and means that you can see the line but not too much lead is left on the paper.

2. Pin the tissue paper onto your background fabric and, using sewing thread, work a line of tacking around the edge.

3. Work rows of running stitch along all the design lines [**A**]. To start and finish the thread, make 2 stitches on top of each other instead of using a knot. This is much more secure when you come to pull the tissue paper away.

A

Seeding stitch is random short stitches scattered across the fabric. These stitches can be placed close together to create a dark tone, or shadow, or stitched wider apart to create a light tone. The final piece looks like it just appears out of the fabric – simple but very effective.

B

4. Once all the design lines have been worked, lift the paper up and, holding the stitching with your finger, gently tear the paper away [B].

5. Place the background fabric and the calico into your hoop, one on top of the other. No need to stitch them together this time as both pieces are large enough to fit in the hoop. Work your way around, pulling the fabric tight. Now tighten the screw to hold the fabric in place — it should feel like a drum.

6. When you are working a whole piece in seeding there is nowhere to hide your starting and finishing stitches. In this case, you can turn your hoop over and work 2 tiny stitches into just the calico. These stitches will not be seen from the front, but will secure the start and finish of your thread [C].

C

7. The diagram opposite is numbered to indicate the level of shade of the area to be worked: ① being the lightest area, with no seeding stitches, and ⑤ being the darkest area, with lots of seeding stitches. Using 2 strands of stranded cotton, begin your seeding stitches in the dark areas, with the stitches very close together [D]. You begin in this way as you can always put fewer stitches in as the areas get lighter, but if you start with the light area and move towards the dark you may run out of room for the number of stitches you need to get the darker effect [E, F].

D

E

F

G

8. When working the lips, work 2 rows of running stitch either side of the centre tacked line before you fill the lips [G]. This will help to slightly separate the top and bottom lips.

9. It is a good idea to look at your work from a distance once in a while to see if the shaded areas are forming the face. You can always add more stitches if an area is not dark enough [H].

10. Once the whole face has been stitched, remove the tacking stitches. Gently slide a needle under the starting or finishing stitches and pull the stitches out one at a time [I]. These may have got caught up with your seeding stitch, if so, just snip the tacking thread close to where it is caught and give it a little pull to free it.

H

I

DIAGRAM FOR SEEDING STITCHES

PROJECT | PICTURE   75

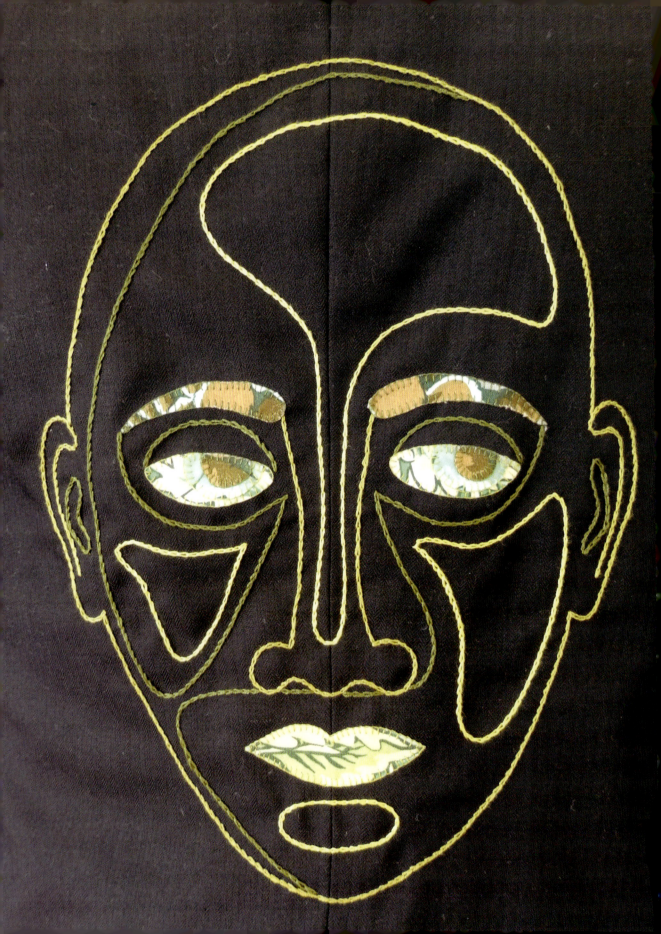

You can often find great suit jackets in second-hand clothes shops; invariably, suit trousers wear out much sooner than the jacket. These suit jackets are often plain dark colours and so are perfect for embelishing with embroidery.

'WATCH YOUR BACK' JACKET

STITCHED AREA
30 x 24cm (11¾ x 9½in)

WHAT YOU NEED
Second-hand suit jacket

Small scraps of fabric for eyes, eyebrows and lips

Fusible web

3 shades of stranded cotton to match your scraps of fabric

Sewing thread for tacking

Size 8 and size 10 embroidery needles

Tracing paper

Transfer paper

STITCHES USED
Chain stitch

Buttonhole stitch

TECHNIQUES
Fusing fabric

> This one-of-a-kind jacket can be created at little cost and will certainly turn heads as you walk down the street. The stitches are basic embroidery stitches; the only thing that makes this project a bit tricky is that the jacket is already made so you don't have a flat fabric to stitch on.

INSTRUCTIONS

1. Enlarge the design on page 79 so that the head is 29cm (11½in) tall and trace it onto tracing paper.

2. Use transfer paper to transfer the design onto the back of your jacket [**A**]. Match the centre line of the design to the seam that runs down the back of the jacket. I tape the design to the transfer paper and then tape the transfer paper to the jacket. This stops anything moving while you are tracing.

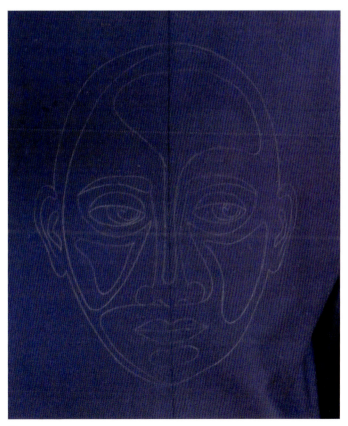

A

INTERMEDIATE

B

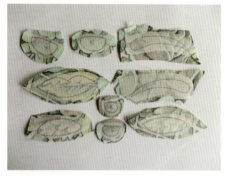

C

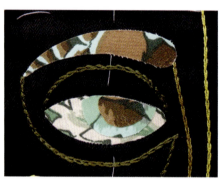

D

3. As the jacket is already made, you will be stitching through the outer fabric and the lining, so you need to tack these layers together to prevent them moving while you embroider.

Tack a grid over the area you will be embroidering – 3 lines across and 4 or 5 lines down the face. This tacking will be removed later so do not worry about the colour of the thread.

4. Using 2 strands of stranded cotton and the size 8 needle, work chain stitch along all your design lines [B].

I have used 3 shades of green stranded cotton — light, medium and dark. I used the medium shade for the main outlines of the face and nose, and the light shade for the highlights on the cheeks, nose and chin. This leaves the dark thread for the shadows under the eyes and beside the nose. Use the main image to help with your colour placement.

Once all the outlines are stitched, it's time to add the features.

5. Flip your tracing of the face over so you are using the back of the design. Trace the eyes, eye brows and lips onto the paper side of your fusible web. The eyes are made up of 3 parts layered on top of one another. It is a good idea to label the eyes and eye brows left and right to help with placement.

6. Cut out each section, leaving a small allowance around the pencil line. This ensures you have a crisp line when you cut these sections out again after they are ironed onto the fabric.

7. Iron your fusible web pieces onto the back of your fabric scraps [C]. I used a single fabric that had a large pattern with areas of light and dark that I could use for the different features, e.g. the dark parts of the pattern were used for the pupils of the eyes. You can use different fabrics to create the tones needed if you wish.

8. Cut your features out along the pencil line and iron in place on the jacket. Layer the 'white', iris and pupil of the eye on top of each other [D].

9. Using 1 strand of stranded cotton and the size 10 needle, work buttonhole stitch around the edge of all your fabric pieces [E].

10. Remove your tacking threads. These may have got caught up with your stitching. If so, just snip the tacking thread close to where it is caught and free it with a little pull.

E

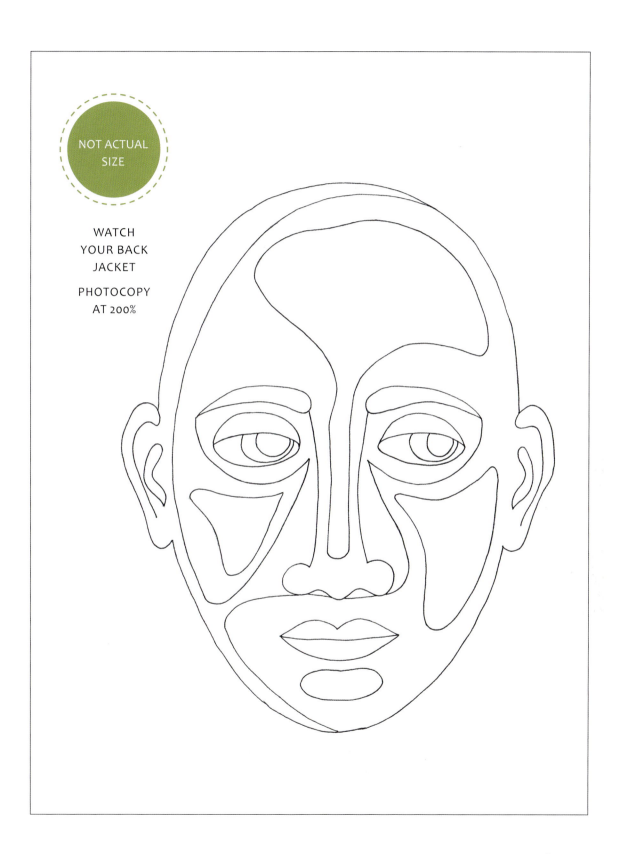

Notebooks with beautiful covers are so much more expensive than the ones with plain covers. So why not buy a plain notebook and embroider your own cover. Then, once the book is used up you can just unpick a few stitches and re-stitch it to a new book. This face design is sized to fit an A5 notebook (21 x 14.8cm or 8¼ x 5¾in), but if your book is larger, you could either have a face that takes up less of the cover or enlarge the design.

'SHADES OF GREEN' BOOK COVER

FINISHED SIZE

22 x 16 cm (8¾ x 6¼in)

WHAT YOU NEED

Background fabric, 55 x 112 cm (21½ x 44in); medium weight, between shirt and denim

Calico, 55 x 55cm (21½ x 21½in)

Stranded cotton, 4 shades; I have used the same colour as my background fabric but a contrast colour would also look striking

Sewing thread to match fabric

Size 8 and size 10 embroidery needles

Embroidery hoop, 25cm (10in)

STITCHES USED

Stem stitch

Long and short stitch

Satin stitch

Back stitch

Over sewing

TECHNIQUES

Transferring design

INSTRUCTIONS

1. Cut your background fabric in half so you have two 55cm (22in) squares.

2. Tack a rectangle 22 x 48cm (8¾ x 19in) in the centre of one of these squares.

3. Transfer the face design on page 85 onto this fabric piece using transfer paper or a light box. The face will sit in the top right corner of your rectangle with the side 7cm (2¾in) in from the end. Do not draw on the straight lines along the top and down the side. (See diagram below.)

4. Making sure your design is sitting within the hoop, place your background fabric and calico into your hoop, work your way around the hoop pulling the fabric tight. Now tighten the screw on your hoop to hold the fabric in place. Your fabric should feel like a drum.

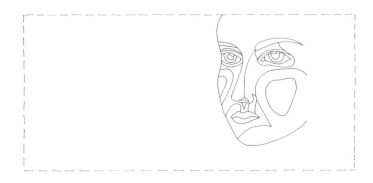

This project combines long and short stitch areas with satin stitch and lines of stem stitch. If you have not done long and short before, please read the long and short instructions on pages 126–127 before you start.

ADVANCED

A

B

C

5. Fill the eyes first, using a mix of long and short stitch and satin stitch. When the area becomes smaller than a short stitch of your long and short, about 1cm (½in), use satin stitch until the area enlarges again.

Using 1 strand of stranded cotton and the size 10 needle start your thread with a knot on the top and 2 small back stitches. Cut the knot off.

Long and short stitch is worked from the background to the foreground (from the most 'behind' element of the design to the most 'in front'). Each area has a split stitch edge around it when the edge is 'on top'. This split stitch is covered up with the long and short stitches [**A–D**].

The diagram below shows the order that you fill the areas of the eye. Use the photo to help with the colours you will choose for your stranded cotton.

D

DIAGRAM SHOWING SHADE OF COTTON NEEDED FOR PARTS OF THE EYES

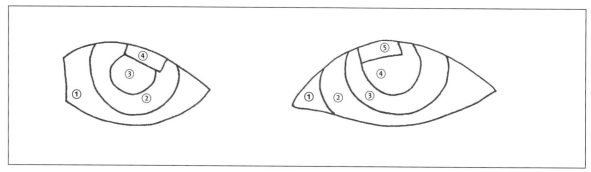

82   STITCH PEOPLE

E

F

G

H

6. The lips are filled with long and short stitches. Beginning with the bottom lip, split stitch just the bottom edge, then fill with long and short.

7. The top lip is next. Split stitch all around the edge of the top lip and fill with long and short stitches [E]. This will make the top lip look as if it is sitting slightly on top of the bottom lip [F].

8. Using 3 strands of your darkest shade of stranded cotton, fill the eyebrow areas with rows of stem stitch, working from the outside to the inside [G, H].

9. Using 3 strands of stranded cotton, work stem stitch along all other design lines. Using the photograph of the finished work to guide your colour choice [I, J]; use darker shades where there would be shadows on the face and lighter shades for the cheeks and outline of the nose.

I

J

PROJECT | BOOK COVER

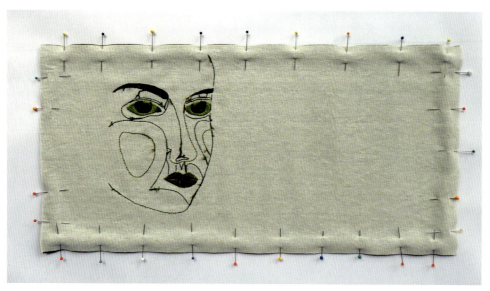

K

L

M

MAKING UP THE BOOK COVER

1. Once the embroidery has been completed, trim both layers of fabric to 1cm (⅜in) outside your tack line. This will be your seam allowance. Remove the tacked line.

2. Cut another piece of fabric the same size from your other background fabric square.

3. With right sides facing, sew these 2 rectangles together either by hand, using back stitch, or by machine. Your sewing line should be 1cm (⅜in) from the edge of the fabric. Leave a 10cm (4in) gap in one of the short sides to allow you to turn your cover right side out [K].

4. Trim a small triangle off each corner without cutting your stitches.

5. Turn right side out and push out the edges and corners To help with this, slightly dampen your finger tips and rub the seams. Use pins to hold this seam while you press it. Close the gap with slip stitch.

6. Lay your book cover face down and place your book in the centre (you will have extra fabric showing at each end).

7. Fold the extra fabric at each end over the book cover. Pin the top and bottom edges together [L].

8. Over sew these edges together firmly by hand [M].

9. When you have filled your notebook, you can then undo the stitches in step 8 and re-use the cover on another book.

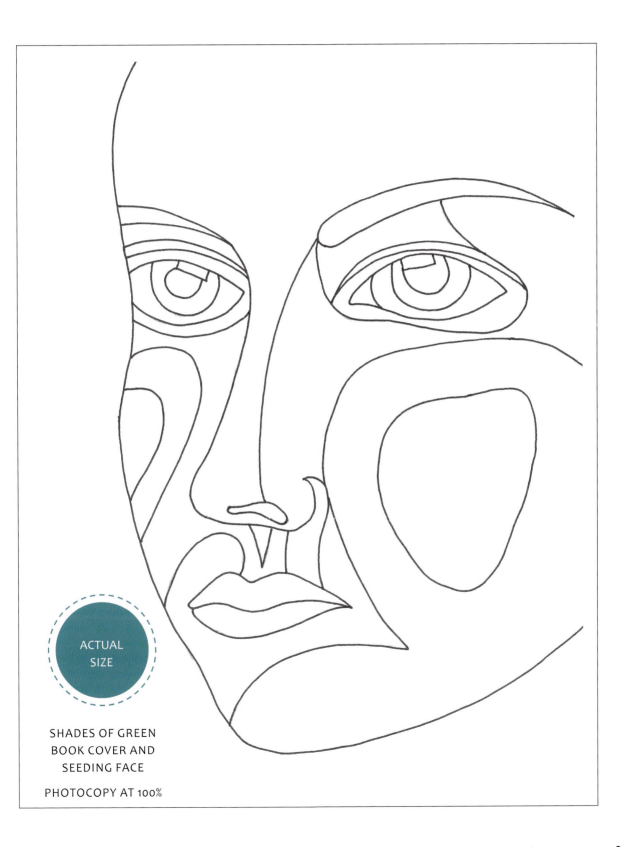

SHADES OF GREEN
BOOK COVER AND
SEEDING FACE

PHOTOCOPY AT 100%

PROJECT | BOOK COVER

I love the idea of covering a high-tech smart phone with a hand-made cover; it turns a piece of technology that looks the same as everyone else's into something that is unique to you. This project is worked mainly in satin stitch with a few areas of long and short stitch where the areas get larger.

'TALK, TALK, TALK' PHONE CASE

ADVANCED

FINISHED SIZE

17 x 10cm (6¾ x 4in)

WHAT YOU NEED

Background fabric, 25 x 25cm (approx. 10 x 10in)

Calico, 50 x 50cm (19¾ x 19¾in)

Lining fabric, 25 x 25cm (approx. 10 x 10in); I used the background fabric again for this

Stranded cotton in a colour that contrasts with the background fabric

Size 10 embroidery needle

Embroidery hoop, 8in (20cm)

STITCHES USED

Split stitch

Long and short stitch

Satin stitch

INSTRUCTIONS

1. Measure your phone and add 1.5cm (⅝in) all around. For example, my phone measures 14 x 7cm (5½ x 2¾in), so the size I need is 17 x 10cm (6¾ x 4in).

2. Draw this rectangle onto your background fabric and cut it out, leaving about 1cm (½in) around the pencil line.

3. Trace the design on page 89 onto the fabric, using transfer paper if your material is dark. The design will remain the same size regardless of the size of your phone; it will just have more or less fabric around it.

4. By hand, using back stitch, or by machine, sew this piece of background fabric onto the centre of your calico square. Keep the stitching line outside the pencil line. The double layer of fabric supports the stitching and also means the calico rather than the fabric goes in the hoop.

5. Place the calico in the hoop, and, working your way around, pull the fabric tight. Then tighten the screw to hold in place. Your fabric should feel like a drum.

6. Using 1 strand of stranded cotton work a split stitch on all the design lines [**A**]. Start your thread with a knot on top and 2 small back stitches on the line, cut the knot off.

> If the areas you are filling with satin stitch are very narrow, i.e. less than 0.5cm (¼in), it is much easier to keep your work neat if the stitches are slanted. As much of this design is narrow, I have kept all the stitches slanted so the overall effect is smooth.

A

PROJECT | CELLPHONE CASE

B

D

E

F

C

7. Many of the areas in this design are narrow, so they will be filled with satin stitch rather than long and short. Bring your needle up on one side of the area, on the outside of the split stitch, and down on the other side, over the split stitch. Come up again on the first side, next to the first stitch [B].

8. When the area get wider and the satin stitch becomes longer than 1cm (½in), start to use long and short stitch [C]. This ensures a smooth finish to the embroidery. Remember to keep the stitches slanted. For the first row of long and short, your stitch will come up in the empty fabric and down over the split stitch. The second row will come up through the stitch of the first row and down over the split stitch on the opposite edge of the area being stitched.

9. Once the embroidery is complete, remove from the hoop and cut the fabric along your pencil line. The calico and background material are treated as one fabric.

10. Cut another piece of background fabric the same size [D]. Pin the two pieces, right sides together, and stitch by hand or by machine, leaving the top open. Your seam allowance is 0.5cm (¼in) [E].

11. Cut two pieces of lining fabric the same size as your background pieces and sew them in the same way as step 10. Trim off the bottom corners of the seam allowance on both the outside case and the lining.

12. Turn the outside of your phone case right side out and push the lining inside.

13. Fold in your 0.5cm (¼in) seam allowance around the top of both the case and the lining and pin [F].

14. Slip stitch around the top.

STITCH PEOPLE

TALK, TALK, TALK PHONE CASE

PHOTOCOPY AT 100%

Lots of people use pin cushions to store their pins. I always store mine in a tin because I imagine the pin cushion saying 'ouch' every time I stick a pin into it! On the other hand, you prick your finger much less often getting pins from a cushion than from a tin. This project is the next step on your 'long and short' journey, with the introduction of two colours. You will practice how to blend the colours together to create shading without a hard line. I think you would find it helpful to read the long and short instructions on pages 126–127 before you start.

'OUCH' PIN CUSHION

PIN CUSHION SIZE

9 x 9cm (3½ x 3½in)

WHAT YOU NEED

Cotton fabric for the background, 18 x 18cm (7 x 7in)

Calico, 40 x 40cm (15¾ x 15¾in)

Stranded cotton, 2 shades of one colour

Size 3 and size 10 embroidery needles

Embroidery hoop, 20cm (8in)

Transfer paper

Toy stuffing

STITCHES USED

Long and short stitch

Trailing (a form of couching)

TECHNIQUES

Simple construction

INSTRUCTIONS

1. Draw the design on page 95 onto your background fabric [A]. If you are using a light colour you can trace through it, but if you material is dark you will need to use transfer paper.

2. Sew your background fabric onto the centre of the calico square by hand using back stitch, or using a sewing machine. This double layer of fabric supports the stitching and saves using your fabric in the hoop.

3. Place the calico into your hoop, and working your way around the hoop, pull the fabric tight. Now tighten the screw to hold it in place. Your fabric should feel like a drum.

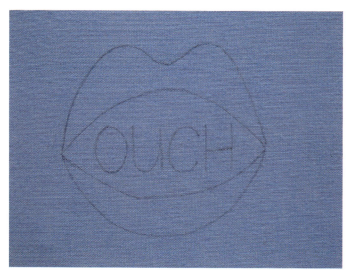

A

ADVANCED

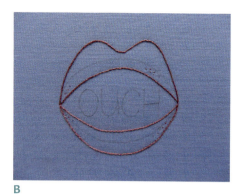

B

C

D

4. Using the lighter of your two shades of lip colour stranded cotton, split stitch around the outside and inside edges of the lips [B].

5. Take the lighter of your lip shades and, starting in the top centre of the top lip, work a first row of long and short stitch. Your longest stitch will be about 1.5cm (⅝in) and your shortest will be about 1cm (½in). Some of these stitches will go over the line that indicates the darker area and some will be within the lighter area. This will ensure you have a blended line rather than a hard line between the light and dark shades of cotton [C].

6. You will need to do two small sections of a second row in the fuller part of the lips – do this in your lighter colour. For these rows, bring your needle up through the stitch of the row before and down into empty fabric [D].

7. When the lighter area of long and short is complete, thread up with the darker shade and work a second row. Start from the centre again and work first one way and then the other [E, F].

E

F

G

H

8. The bottom lip will start with the darker colour. This is because long and short is easier to work from the top of an area. Working from the centre again, work a first row in the darker colour and then a second row in the lighter shade [G].

9. Once the lips have been worked, you are ready to stitch the letters [H].

10. Using your darker coloured stranded cotton you will work the letters in trailing. This is a very close together couching. Use all 6 strands of stranded cotton as your base thread and 1 strand to couch over. The couching stitches should be so close together that you cannot see the base thread [I].

I

11. Cut a length of stranded cotton 55cm (21½in) long. This will be your base thread. Use 1 strand and your size 10 needle to couch this down. Start your thread with a knot and 2 small stitches on the pencil line, then cut your knot off. Leave a 5cm (2in) length of base thread hanging free at the start of your first letter.

At the end of each letter or section of a letter, thread the base thread into your size 3 needle, take it through to the reverse of the work and bring it back up at the start of the next letter [J]. The U and the H are worked in 2 or 3 sections, the curve of the U first then the straight side [K]. For the H, work one straight side, then the middle, then the other side.

J

K

PROJECT | PIN CUSHION

L

M

N

12. When you have completed all the letters, take the start and finish ends through to the reverse of the work and stitch the ends to the back of the fabric for about 2cm (¾in) to secure. Cut off the remaining thread [L].

13. Cut the stitched piece into a 10 x 10cm (4 x 4in) square, along with another piece of fabric the same size. I have used a contrast colour for the back.

14. Pin these 2 pieces right sides together and sew around the outside edge, leaving a gap in the centre of one side [M].

15. Turn right side out and stuff with toy stuffing.

16. Sew up the gap using slip stitch [N].

OUCH
PIN CUSHION

PHOTOCOPY
AT 100%

Stitch samplers have been used to learn and practice stitches for years. This is a contemporary take on that idea, and while you practice your stitches, you are creating an interesting piece to hang on your wall.

'BUS QUEUE' STITCH SAMPLER

STITCHED AREA

15 x 26cm (6 x 10¼in)

WHAT YOU NEED

Background fabric, 50 x 50cm (19¾ x 19¾in), plain cotton
Calico, 50 x 50cm (19¾ x 19¾in)
Embroidery hoop, 30.5cm (12in)
Selection of stranded cotton
Size 8 and size 10 embroidery needles

STITCHES USED

Back stitch, Seeding, Satin stitch, Feather stitch, Fly stitch, Long and short stitch, Herringbone stitch, Stem stitch, Chain stitch, Split stitch

> This project uses some stitches you have come across in the earlier projects in this book, e.g. back stitch, seeding, stem stitch, chain stitch and satin stitch, but it will introduce you to a few more decorative stitches – feather, fly and herringbone stitches. Instructions for all of these can be found in the Stitch Gallery, pages 118–125.

STITCH PEOPLE

ADVANCED

A

B

C

INSTRUCTIONS

1. Trace the design on page 103 onto the background fabric using either a light box or transfer paper [**A**].

2. Place your background fabric on top of your calico and place both fabrics together in your hoop. The calico supports the background fabric and helps prevent wrinkles around the stitched areas. Work your way around the hoop, pulling the fabric tight. Now tighten the screw to hold it in place. Your fabric should feel like a drum. The design will take up a large part of the hoop, so it is best to have a whole piece of background fabric in the hoop, rather than the small piece stitched to calico as in previous projects. Where possible, you should use a hoop large enough to contain the complete design. If you are using a smaller hoop, you will need to stitch a section of the design and then move your hoop.

3. Each area and outline of the people is stitched using a different coloured thread and/or a different stitch.

It is best to fill an area before you work the outline stitch as this enables you to start and end your thread along the pencil line which is then covered with another stitch [**B**].

4. The diagram on page 102 shows which stitch is used for which area. The filling stitches are feather, herringbone, fly, seeding, long and short and satin. All are worked in 1 strand of stranded cotton and a size 10 needle. The outlines are working in chain, stem and back stitch using 2 strands of stranded cotton and a size 8 needle. The instructions for all these stitches are in the stitch gallery (pages 118–127).

5. The feather stitch on the first dress on the left changes size as it goes down the body. Start at the top neck edge with a knot and 2 small stitches on the outline. The centre line of the feather stitch will be an imagined line, or you can lightly draw it on with a pencil. This line will be half way between the arm and the outline of the clothes. On this centre line, bring your needle up on the neck edge. Then put your needle down through the fabric, either on the outline of the garment or the outline of the arm. As you progress down the garment the stitches will get larger, but that's fine. When you reach the hem of the dress you can fill the spaces that will be left, due to the shape of the stitch, with straight stitches [**C**].

6. All the bags, the green hat and most of the shoes are worked using satin stitch or long and short stitch [**D–H**].

D

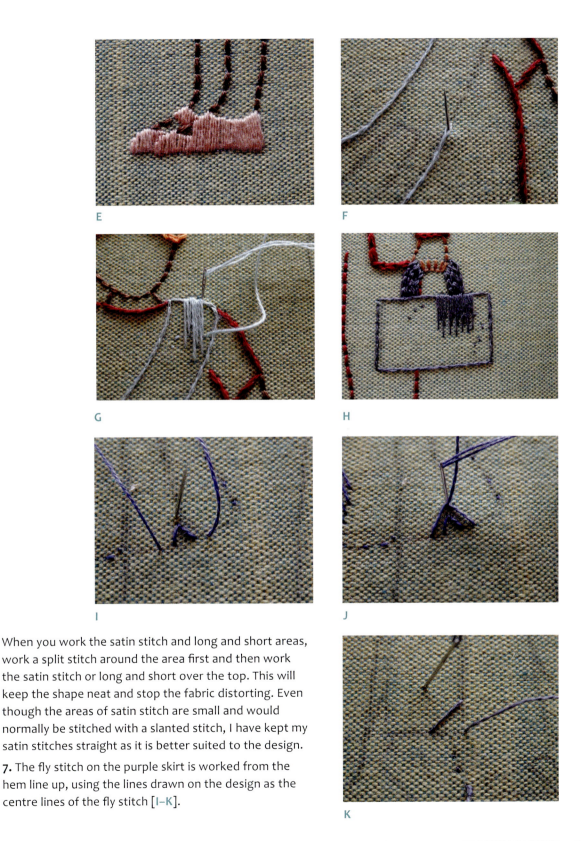

E

F

G

H

I

J

When you work the satin stitch and long and short areas, work a split stitch around the area first and then work the satin stitch or long and short over the top. This will keep the shape neat and stop the fabric distorting. Even though the areas of satin stitch are small and would normally be stitched with a slanted stitch, I have kept my satin stitches straight as it is better suited to the design.

7. The fly stitch on the purple skirt is worked from the hem line up, using the lines drawn on the design as the centre lines of the fly stitch [I–K].

K

PROJECT | SAMPLER   99

L

8. Herringbone stitch is used for the grey trousers and the green scarf. The grey trousers are worked in rows of herringbone stitch. Imagine a line that divides each leg in half. Use this imagined line to guide the size of your stitches. The lines of the scarf you drew on in step 1 are used to guide the width of each section of stitching [L, M].

9. There are 2 small areas of seeding – a bag flap [N] and a t-shirt. These are worked using 2 strands of stranded cotton even though they are a filling stitch because seeding looks better with a slightly thicker thread.

M

10. When you come to your outlines, you cannot stitch around a sharp corner with chain stitch or stem stitch. You have to stop at the corner and start a new line of stitches.

I have used back stitch to give a finer outline for faces, hands and legs [O]. Chain stitch and stem stitch give a thicker outline, so I have used those for the clothes [P–U].

11. The orange hat and the soles of the red boots are filled with rows of chain stitch [V, W].

12. Using the diagram on page 102 as a guide, work 3 rows of running stitch on the trousers of the last person in the queue [X]. These lines are not drawn on beforehand as running stitch will not cover the drawn line.

N

O

P

PROJECT | SAMPLER 101

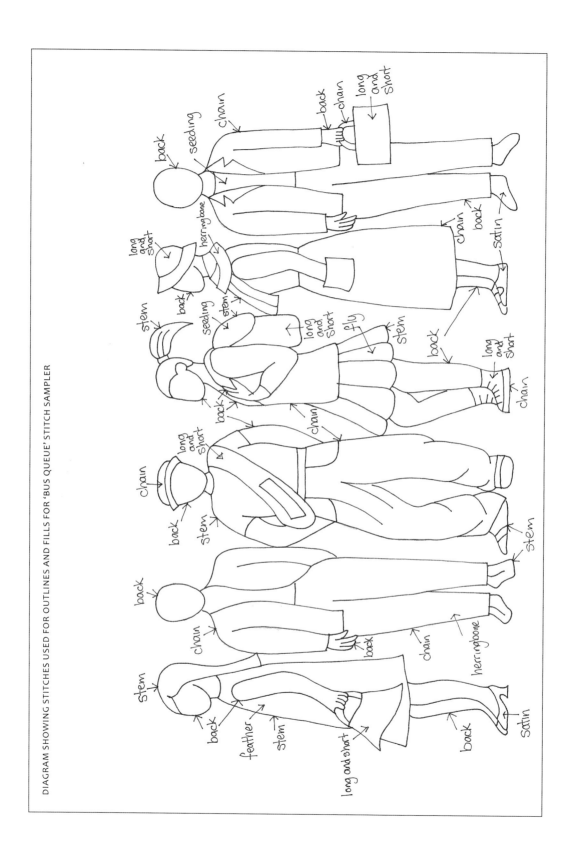

DIAGRAM SHOWING STITCHES USED FOR OUTLINES AND FILLS FOR 'BUS QUEUE' STITCH SAMPLER

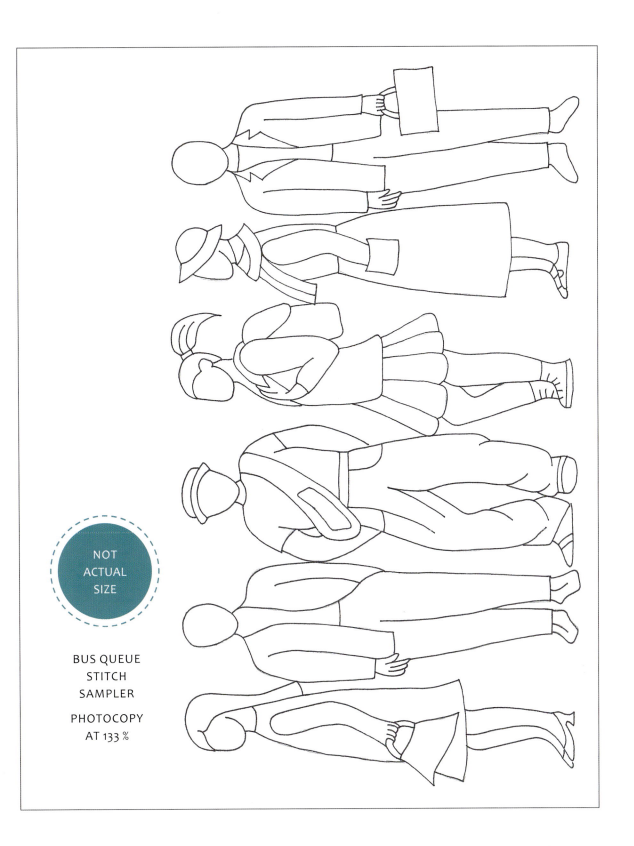

BUS QUEUE STITCH SAMPLER

PHOTOCOPY AT 133%

NOT ACTUAL SIZE

The idea of seeing a face in the shadows of the moon has been a subject of art for many years. I like to think of the 'Man in the Moon' as a friendly face looking out for us. With this stitched brooch, you can carry that friendly soul with you wherever you go. Before you start, I suggest you stitch 'Moving but Still' on page 68. This will give you experience in couching in rows using metal thread, so that in this project you will only be learning the techniques of changing your thread colour and stitch spacing.

'MAN IN THE MOON' BROOCH

FINISHED MEASUREMENTS

5.5 x 5.5cm (2¼ x 2¼in)

WHAT YOU NEED

Calico, 30 x 30cm (11¾ x 11¾in)

Silver passing, 7m (23ft)

Stranded cotton in 2 shades of grey, mid grey and dark grey

Size 3 and size 10 embroidery needles

Embroidery hoop, 20cm (8in)

STITCHES USED

Or nue, a type of couching

INSTRUCTIONS

1. Trace your design onto the calico by placing the design underneath and tracing through. Draw on the outline and the lines within the face to show the shaded areas [A].

2. Place the calico into your hoop and, working your way around, pull the fabric tight. Now tighten the screw to hold it in place. Your fabric should feel like a drum.

A

This project will introduce you to 'or nue'. Or nue is a metal thread technique that involves the couching of a metal thread with different colours to produce a picture or design. The couching threads can be put close together or farther apart to produce a shaded effect. Couching as a stitch is not hard, but the changing of colour and shading take some thought and it is time-consuming — this piece will not be finished in a day! Changing the direction of the metal thread enables the light to fall on it differently and bring the piece to life.

ADVANCED +

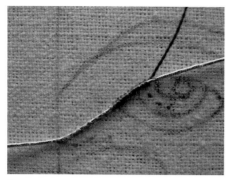

B

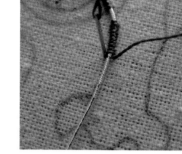

C

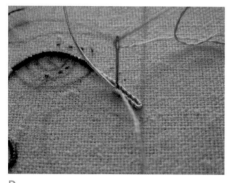

D

E

F

3. Your first line of couching will follow the line of the top of the eyes and around the nose. Leave a 4cm (1½in) length of your metal passing thread hanging free at the side of the square.

Start with the lighter grey stranded cotton and the couching stitches close together but with small gaps of metal showing through. When you come to the pencil line of the eye, change to the darker shade and couch the metal with a solid line of stitches, i.e. no metal showing through [B]. There will be a small gap of metal as you turn the passing thread and work down the outline of the nose [C].

This first line continues across the face to the opposite side, where you turn your metal to either go above the eyes or below. It will make no difference whether you go above or below. I have gone below [D].

4. Continue to work rows of couching, following this first line, until the face is full. When you come to a pencil line that you have drawn on the calico, you have to make a decision. This will either be to change to the other shade of couching thread or to make your stitches closer together or farther apart [E, F]. Use the image of the finished face to help with this.

The outlines are all couched very close together with your darker shade. The shadows around the nose and under the eyes are couched in the lighter shade quite close together. Small gaps of metal thread will show and the lighter areas of the face have larger gaps of metal showing through.

G

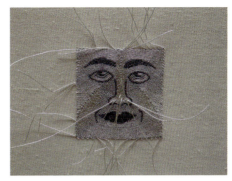

H

5. Whenever you get to the edge of your square, turn the metal and go back the way you have just come from. You will also need to turn the metal within the face when the areas get too narrow.

To turn the metal thread, you need to work a couching stitch at the end of the row, then bend the metal thread against this stitch and pinch. You can use a pair of tweezers to do this.

When working couching in rows, always bring your needle up on the fabric side and down next to the previous row as this pulls the rows closer together.

The diagram on page 109 gives you an idea of how the rows will look. This is not exact, as everyone has a different stitching tension so the number of rows will differ from person to person.

I

6. When I stitch this design, I find it easier to have two needles threaded up, one with each shade. You can bring these up to rest on the top of your hoop when you are not using them. Do not leave them hanging at the back, as you will get in a huge tangle under your frame.

7. Due to the shape of the rows, you will end up with small areas that will need to be filled in separately. Always remember to leave a 4cm (1½in) length of passing thread at the start and end of each area [G, H].

8. Once your whole face has been completed, use a size 3 needle to pull your start and finish ends through to the back [I].

9. Couch these ends to the stitches on the back side of the work [J, K].

J

K

PROJECT | BROOCH

L

M

N

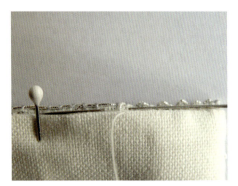

O

10. Cut around the face leaving 1cm (½in) of calico all around [L].

11. The metal stitching is so firm that you can just fold the calico along the edge and sew to the back side of the stitching [M, N].

12. Cut a piece of calico, 6.5 x 6.5cm (2½ x 2½in). You will have some left after you have cut out the finished or nue. Fold over and press 0.5cm (¼in) all around and slip stitch to the back of your brooch to cover up all your ends [O].

13. Sew your brooch pin to the back of your piece.

MAN IN
THE MOON
OR NUE
BROOCH

PHOTOCOPY
AT 100%

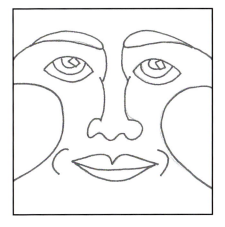

DIAGRAM SHOWING LINES OF COUCHING

I have always loved looking at stone carvings, and, of course, faces and bodies are my favourite subjects. This project takes this concept and introduces shading with long and short stitch, sometimes called silk shading or needle painting. The secret is keeping your stitches long and uneven, which gives the smooth, shaded finish.

'STONY-FACED' LONG AND SHORT PICTURE

STITCHED AREA

7 x 7cm (2¾ x 2¾in)

WHAT YOU NEED

Background fabric, 20 x 20cm (8 x 8in); I have used patchwork cotton but silk would be fine too. A light to medium tone is best as dark colours are harder to cover with thread

Calico, 40 x 40cm (15¾ x 15¾in)

Stranded cotton, 6 shades from very light to very dark. In the instructions I have numbered the colours 1 (lightest), to 6 (darkest)

Size 10 embroidery needle

Embroidery hoop, 20cm (8in)

STITCHES USED

Long and short

Split stitch

Satin stitch

INSTRUCTIONS

1. Trace the design on page 115 onto your background fabric. You should be able to do this with a light box or using a window [A].

2. Sew your background fabric onto the centre of your calico square by hand, using back stitch, or with a sewing machine. You need a double layer of fabric to support the stitching and this saves your background fabric from being used in the hoop.

3. Place the calico into your hoop and work your way around, pulling the fabric tight. Now tighten the screw to hold it in place. Your fabric should feel like a drum.

For this piece, all the stitches will be straight up and down, this is sometimes called tapestry shading (you can draw some lines onto the fabric to help keep your stitches straight).

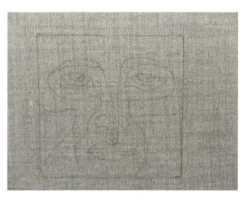

A

The long and short projects in this book build up your knowledge of the stitch and slowly introduce the technique of shading, using, at first, two colours. I strongly recommend you stitch some of the other long and short projects before you try this face, and re-read the long and short instructions on pages 126–127. Even though we had amazing teachers when I was training at the Royal School of Needlework, it took me two years to truly master long and short stitch. So keep trying and you will get there.

B

C

D

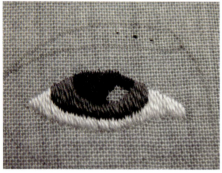

E

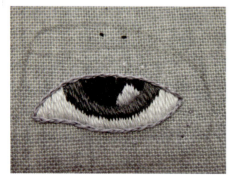

F

Just as a reminder: Within your rows of long and short all the stitches are different lengths, and when you move down to stitch the next row your needle comes up through the end of the stitch of the row before and down into empty fabric. Whenever there is a split stitch, your needle goes over it.

4. The first area to be worked are the eyes. If you think about your eye, the lids are on top of your eyes and your iris is on top of the white of the eye. As you always work from the 'back' of a design to the foreground, the whites of the eye are worked first, in colour 1. No edges of this area are 'on top' so no split stitch is needed. The area is small, so it is filled with satin stitch [B, C].

5. Next is the iris, worked in colour 5. A split stitch is worked around the bottom edge of this area, where it is 'on top' of the white of the eye. Then the area is filled with satin stitch [D].

6. Next is the pupil, in colour 6, with split stitch around the bottom. Last is the highlight, in colour 2, which has a split stitch all around [E, F].

7. The long and short that fills the face is worked from the top of each area down. Because the eye brows, nose and lips are 'on top' of the face you leave a gap for these when you work the face as you will return to fill them later.

G

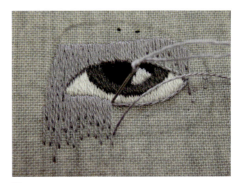

H

8. I have started with colour 4 for the shadow around the eye. A split stitch is worked around the eye, as the skin is 'on top' of the eye, and then the long and short is started below the eyebrow and worked down to the eye [G]. Then one row is worked from the bottom of the eye down the face [H].

9. The shading lines marked on the design are a guide to where to change your colour. The long and short stitches sometimes go over this line and sometimes stop short. This blends the threads of different shades together, creating a smooth effect [I].

10. Once you have filled the space between the eyebrow and eye and one row of long and short from the bottom of the eye, you then start filling the face from the very top edge [J].

11. Work rows of long and short down to the eyebrow and from below the eye down the cheeks. Taking note of the shade lines to remind you to change colour [K].

I

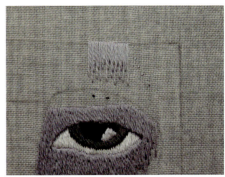

J

K

PROJECT | PICTURE

L

M

N

O

P

Q

12. Once the face has been filled, move onto the nose. Work a split stitch around the outline of the nose [L] and then fill with colour 2. You will blend these stitches with the rows of long and short you have already worked for the forehead [M].

13. The lips are next. Work the bottom lip first with a split stitch around just the bottom edge, then fill with a mix of long and short and satin stitch in colour 5 [N].

14. Split stitch all around the top lip and fill with a mix of long and short and satin stitch in colour 5 [O].

15. The eyebrows are last. Work these in colour 5. Split stitch around the edge and fill with satin stitch [P, Q].

16. This piece will have taken you some time to stitch, so take it to a picture framer and have it put in a frame worthy of your efforts!

STONY-FACED
LONG & SHORT
PICTURE

PHOTOCOPY AT
100%

DIAGRAM SHOWING SHADING GUIDE

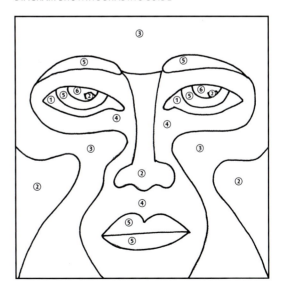

STITCH GALLERY

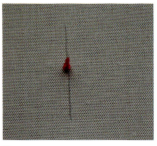

A

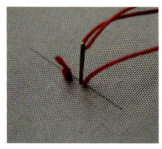

B

To start a thread and end a thread

1. Tie a knot at the end of your thread.

2. Place this knot on top of the fabric about 2cm (¾in) from where the stitching will start [**A**].

3. Work 2 small back stitches along the line or within the area that will be worked, moving towards the starting point [**B, C**].

4. Cut the knot off.

You can end a thread with 2 small back stitches, then cut off the thread.

This way there are no knots at the back of your work.

C

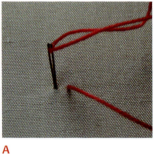

A

B

Running stitch

1. Bring your needle up at the start of the line to be stitched.

2. Take your needle down a stitch length away, about 0.5cm (¼in) [**A**]. This size can vary relative to the thickness of your thread; thin thread can have a smaller stitch than thick thread.

3. Bring your needle up again a stitch length away and repeat. The gap between the stitches should be about the same size as the stitch [**B**].

4. When working with fabric that is not in a hoop, you can do steps A and B at the same time [**C**].

Running stitch is also used for **tacking/basting** fabrics together, but when tacking the stitch length is much longer.

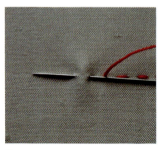

C

Back stitch

1. Bring your needle up a stitch length, 0.5cm (¼in), away from the start of the line to be stitched.

2. Take your needle down at the start of the line [A].

3. Bring your needle up a stitch length away from the end of the first stitch [B].

4. Take your needle down at the end of the first stitch, and repeat along the line to be stitched [C].

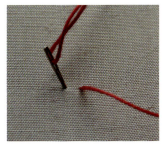
A

B

C

Stem stitch

1. Bring your needle up at the start of the line you wish to stitch.

2. Take your needle down a stitch length away, 0.5cm (¼in). Do not pull the thread all the way down but hold it to one side.

3. Bring your needle up half way between each end of this stitch, pull the thread firm [A].

4. Take another stitch, hold the thread to the same side as before.

5. Bring the needle up at the end of the previous stitch, pull the thread firm [B].

The reason you hold the loop to one side when you bring the needle up is to ensure you don't split the thread. The end result looks similar to a twisted rope.

A

B

Seeding stitch

A

Seeding stitch is individual running stitches worked at different angles to fill a space. Bring your needle up and down about 0.5cm (¼in) apart randomly across your fabric [A].

Chain stitch

A

B

C

D

1. Bring your needle up and down at the start of the line you wish to stitch [A].

2. Hold the loop of thread with your finger.

3. Bring the needle up through the loop a stitch length, 0.5cm (¼in), from the start [B].

4. Pull the thread firm.

5. Take the needle down, through the loop, at the same point as you came up [C].

6. Hold the loop with your finger.

7. Bring the needle up through the loop a stitch length away [D].

8. To end the line of chain stitch, work a small stitch over the end of the last chain to hold it in place [E].

E

Herringbone stitch

1. Bring the needle up on the top edge of the area to be filled.

2. Take the needle down to the bottom edge on an angle. Pull the thread firm [**A**].

3. Bring the needle up in line with where you went down, halfway between the start and end of the first stitch [**B**].

4. Take the needle down on the top edge now, again at an angle. This forms the 'x' on the bottom edge [**C**].

5. Bring the needle up in line with where you went down, level with the bottom 'x'.

6. Take the needle down on the bottom edge, this forms the 'x' on the top edge [**D**].

The back of herringbone stitch looks like two lines of running stitch.

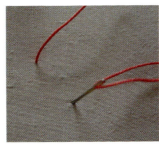
A

B

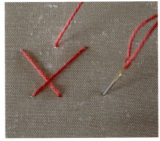
C

D

Couching

1. Start your couching thread along the line to be covered (I have used a contrasting colour in the photographs so that you can see the stitches clearly). Lay the thread to be couched onto the surface of the fabric leaving a 5cm (2in) tail beyond the end of the line.

2. Bring your needle up on one side of this thread, at the start of the line you are couching [**A**].

3. Take the needle down the other side of the couched thread and pull the thread firm [**B**].

4. Repeat this at intervals of about 0.5cm (¼in), along the couched thread.

5. When you have finished, thread the couched threads onto a large needle and pull through to the back of your work [**C**].

6. Over-sew ends to the back of the work.

A

B

C

A

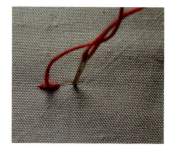

B

Split stitch

1. Take a stitch and pull the thread firm.

2. Bring the needle up through the middle of this stitch, splitting the thread [**A**].

3. Take a stitch and pull the thread firm [**B, C**].

4. Continue along the line to be stitched [**D**].

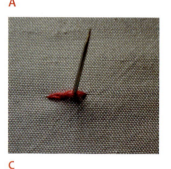

C

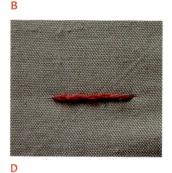

D

A

B

Feather stitch

1. Bring the needle up in the centre at the top of the line you wish to stitch.

2. Take the needle down to the side, hold this loop with your finger [**A**].

3. Bring the needle up on the centre line, through the loop, a stitch length away from where you first came up, 0.5cm (¼in), and pull the thread firm [**B**].

4. Take the needle down on the other side, hold the loop [**C**].

5. Bring needle up on the centre line, through the loop and pull the thread firm [**D**].

6. When you come to the end of the line, secure the final loop with a small stitch over the end, in the same way as chain stitch.

C

D

Satin stitch

1. Work a split stitch around the edge of the area you wish to satin stitch [**A**].

2. Bring your needle up on the outside edge of the split stitch, at the top of the area to be worked [**B**].

3. Take the needle down straight across the shape to the outside edge of the split stitch [**C**].

4. Bring the needle back up at the top, next to the first stitch [**D**].

5. Work in this way from the centre to one side of the area, then go back to the centre and work out to the other side [**E**].

The split stitch becomes completely covered.

When the area you wish to fill is larger than 1cm (½in) you would use long and short stitch (see pages 126–127) instead of satin stitch. Satin stitches become unstable when they get too long. Long and short and satin stitches are often used together to fill an area.

Note: When an area is a narrow strip satin stitch is easier to work on an angle.

A

B

C

D

E

Fly stitch

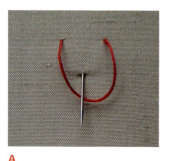

A

B

Fly stitch is worked in a similar way to chain stitch but there is a gap between where you come up and down forming a 'V' rather than an 'O'.

1. Bring your needle up at the top of the line you wish to stitch.

2. Take the needle down at the same level but with a space in between, hold the loop of thread in your hand.

3. Bring the needle up again through the loop, at a point below the first stitch and in the centre [**A**].

4. Pull the stitch firm to form a 'V' shape.

5. Take the needle down over the point of the 'V' to hold the stitch in place [**B**].

Slip stitch

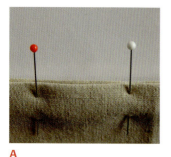

A

B

C

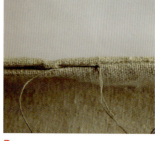

D

Slip stitch is a method of joining two pieces of fabric that have a seam allowance folded under. It is mostly used for stitching linings into bags, backings onto hangings or fabric appliqué with a folded under edge.

1. Pin the two fabrics wrong sides together, matching the folded edges [**A**].

2. Tie a knot in the end of your thread and slide your needle inside to come out on the fold of one of the fabrics (the knot is hidden inside) [**B**].

3. Take the thread across to the other fabric and slide the needle into the fold and along about 0.5cm (¼in) and out again [**C**].

4. Bring the thread back to the first fabric and repeat [**D**].

Where you come out of one fabric and go into the other fabric will be exactly in line so the stitches do not show.

Buttonhole stitch

Buttonhole stitch is often used around the edge of appliqué, but can also be used as a decorative stitch as part of an embroidery design.

1. Bring your needle up through the background fabric, on the edge of the top fabric, or on the line you wish to cover.

2. Take the needle down a stitch length above this point, 0.5cm (¼in), at a slight angle. Hold the thread and don't pull it tight [**A**].

3. Bring your needle up again on your line or the edge of your fabric, through the loop of thread, and pull the thread firm [**B**].

4. Take the needle down again above this point, at an angle [**C**].

5. When you have come to the end of your line, the last loop is held down with a small stitch over the thread, the same as for chain stitch [**D**].

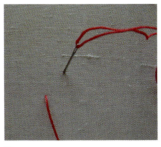
A

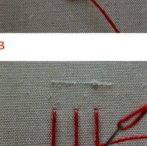
B

C

D

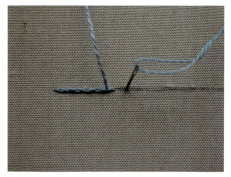

A

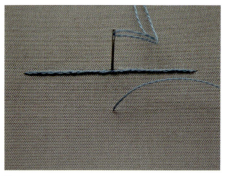

B

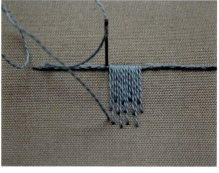

C

Long and short stitch

Long and short is a fantastic smooth, dense stitch that will fill large or small areas with or without shading. It is sometimes called silk shading or needle painting. All the long and short projects in this book are worked with the stitches straight, i.e. no change of direction. This is sometimes called tapestry shading. This is really just an introduction to long and short, but it may lead to an ongoing passion for the stitch.

When I was first introduced to this stitch at the Royal School of Needlework, I stressed over every stitch and really struggled to get a smooth result. Once I learned to relax, the whole flow of the stitch improved and the end result was much smoother. It takes practice to keep your stitches straight and smooth, so do not panic if you find this stitch difficult to begin with. Keep working at it and you will improve. It took me two years to feel happy with my long and short; if you have just started, you have plenty of time.

Within a design, the areas of long and short are worked from the most 'behind' element of the design to the most 'on top'. A split stitch is worked around each area as you go.

First split stitch around the area, then long and short, then split stitch the next area. Note that only the edges of the area that will be 'on top' are split stitched. Each long and short project in this book has an order of work list to help you with this. The split stitch keeps the edge neat and holds the grain of the fabric in place so the fabric does not distort as you stitch. Your long and short will completely cover this stitch, but work it in the same thread just in case there is a small gap in your long and short. If an area is very small, fill it with satin stitch.

- -

1. Work a split stitch exactly on your drawn line, on the edge of your first area [**A**]. Remember, only edges that are 'on top' get a split stitch. Your first area to be filled may be 'behind' everything so will not have a split stitch.

Once the split stitch has been completed, your long and short is worked in rows across the area, starting from the centre top.

2. Starting with a long stitch, approximately 1.5cm (⅝in) long, bring your needle up inside the area and straight down over the top of the split stitch [**B**].

D

3. Your next stitch will be shorter. Again bring your needle up inside the shape and down over the split stitch. This stitch will sit next to the first stitch, with no gap [C].

4. Your first row is the only row where your stitches are both long and short, but even then, all your long stitches will be slightly different lengths, as will all your short stitches. The shortest the stitch will be close to 1cm (⅜in).

5. Continue to work out from the centre, alternating longer and shorter stitches until you come to the side. Then return to the centre by either jumping across the back if you have thread remaining or starting a new thread and completing the row the other way. You will have a smooth edge over your split stitch and an uneven edge within your area.

6. To start the next row return to the centre. All the stitches from now on are long stitches, but all slightly different lengths [D].

7. The stitches are now worked by bringing the needle up through the thread of the stitch in the previous row – splitting the stitch about one-third of the way up from the bottom – and down into the empty fabric. Because your first row had uneven stitch lengths, so your next row will have uneven stitch lengths. This means that your long and short will be smooth, with no visible rows [E].

8. When you start to shade within your long and short areas, you leave gaps in one colour that are filled with the next colour. Your eye will then blend those two threads together to create a smooth change from one colour to the next [F]. Always complete each row before you move on to the next.

As you move down your area the rows start to become less defined. This is the effect you want – no visible rows equals a smooth finish [G].

9. Once your first area has been filled, you then split stitch around the next area and fill that with long and short. Continue in this way, working from the most 'behind' area to the most 'on top', until your whole piece is filled.

Things to remember when you are working long and short stitch:

- If there is a split stitch your needle goes down over it.
- If there is a long or short stitch your needle comes up through it.

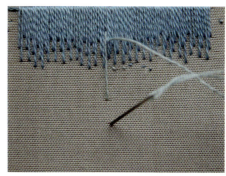

E

F

G